RUDOLF STEINER (1861–1925) called his spiritual philosophy 'anthroposophy', meaning 'wisdom of the human being'. As a highly developed seer, he based his work on direct knowledge and perception of spiritual dimensions. He initiated a modern and universal 'science of spirit', accessible to anyone willing to exercise clear and unprejudiced thinking.

From his spiritual investigations Steiner provided suggestions for the renewal of many activities, including education (both general and special), agriculture, medicine, economics, architecture, science, philosophy, religion and the arts. Today there are thousands of schools, clinics, farms and other organizations involved in practical work based on his principles. His many published works feature his research into the spiritual nature of the human being, the evolution of the world and humanity, and methods of personal development. Steiner wrote some 30 books and delivered over 6000 lectures across Europe. In 1924 he founded the General Anthroposophical Society, which today has branches throughout the world.

MANIFESTATIONS OF KARMA

*Eleven lectures given in Hamburg
between 16 and 28 May 1910*

RUDOLF STEINER

RUDOLF STEINER PRESS

Translation revised by Heidi Herrmann-Davey

Rudolf Steiner Press
Hillside House, The Square
Forest Row RH18 5ES

www.rudolfsteinerpress.com

First edition 1924, private printing
Second edition 1936, Rudolf Steiner Publishing Company, London
Reprinted 1947, 1969, 1976
Third edition 1994, Rudolf Steiner Press, Bristol
Fourth edition 1995, Rudolf Steiner Press, London
Fifth edition 2000, reprinted 2004, 2011

Originally published in German under the title *Die Offenbarungen des Karma*
(volume 120 in the *Rudolf Steiner Gesamtausgabe* or Collected Works) by
Rudolf Steiner Verlag, Dornach. This authorized translation published by
kind permission of the Rudolf Steiner Nachlassverwaltung, Dornach

A catalogue record for this book is available from the British Library

ISBN 978 1 85584 058 4

Cover by Andrew Morgan Design
Typeset by Imprint Publicity Service, Crawley Down, Sussex
Printed and bound by Gutenberg Press, Malta

CONTENTS

FOREWORD

Traditional interpretations of human destiny or karma rest on the assumption that the human being's cognitive powers either cannot, or else must not, penetrate to the deeper mysteries of existence, to an understanding of the laws of karma. Rudolf Steiner has shown that it is possible and indeed essential for human beings to become aware of karma today.

The lectures in this book were given in 1910, to an audience familiar with the fundamental concepts of spiritual science. Rudolf Steiner had already described the laws of reincarnation and karma in several of his written works as well as detailing a clear path towards gaining knowledge of the higher worlds through self-transformation. In the *Manifestations of Karma* lectures he gives illustrative examples of the workings of karma which reveal the interweaving of individual personal karma with the karma of larger groups of people and ultimately that of humanity as a whole.

We fashion our destiny in accordance with the insights gained between death and a new birth. Consequently certain things will happen to us of necessity. How we respond to these in our earthly life is a matter of our individual freedom and will determine our future karma.

Karmic awareness is the key to attaining greater freedom in the choices we make. The implications of this are somewhat wider than suggested by the emphasis some contemporary notions of spirituality place on personal fulfilment or self-redemption.

By exploring the more hidden aspects of a whole range of

life phenomena in the light of the evolution of our planet Rudolf Steiner raises our consciousness to the vital role we play in helping or hindering the powers which serve the world's evolvement.

Heidi Herrmann-Davey

LECTURE 1 ✳

The Nature and Significance of Karma in Humanity, the Earth and the Universe

Hamburg, 16 May 1910

In this cycle of lectures we will deal with various questions of spiritual science which are extremely important to our lives. As I have already pointed out on many occasions spiritual science is not an abstract theory, a mere doctrine or teaching; it is a source of life and fitness for life and fulfils its task only when the knowledge it can impart pours something into our souls which makes life richer, enhances our understanding of life and makes us more competent and effective. This is something you will all be familiar with. However, if you look around you to find out how such ideals might be applied in life you might feel disheartened. For if we consider impartially what the world thinks it 'knows' today, and what makes people feel or act in one way or another today, we might well conclude that all of this is much too far removed from anthroposophical ideas and ideals for the anthroposophist to influence life directly by what he has acquired from spiritual science. Yet such a view would be rather superficial since it takes no account of what we ourselves need to learn. If the forces we develop through anthroposophy really do become sufficiently strong they will find ways of working in the world; whereas if no efforts were ever made to strengthen these forces it would be impossible to make a difference in the world. But there is something else which may comfort us when we are in danger of losing heart, and this is the very purpose of what I am going to deal with in this cycle of lectures – the subject of karma in human life and in general. For with every hour we spend here we shall see more clearly that there is no end to what we can do to make anthroposophy work in the world; we shall also see how karma itself will bring us what we need to do in the short or long term to develop our forces, as long as we seriously believe in it. We shall also understand the following: whenever we believe that we cannot yet apply the forces gained from our view of the world, it is simply a question of our not having developed these forces sufficiently for karma to enable us to work in the world with them. In other words, these lectures will do more than build up a body of knowledge about karma; in every hour our confidence in karma will be more fully awakened, and we shall have the certainty that when the time comes – be it tomorrow or the day after or in many years' time – our karma will bring us the tasks which we, as anthroposophists, may need to perform. Karma will reveal itself to us as a teaching which not only tells us how different things in the world relate to one another, but will make our lives more satisfying and rich.

But if karma is really to do this we must go more deeply into its laws and its working in the universe. In this case, it is to a certain extent necessary that I should do something unusual for me in dealing with questions of spiritual science, namely, to give a definition, an explanation, of a word. I don't normally do this, as explanations of words are usually not very useful. In our considerations we generally begin by the presentation of facts, and if these facts are grouped and arranged in the proper way, the concepts and ideas follow of themselves; but if we were to follow a similar course with regard to the comprehensive questions which we have to discuss during the next few lectures, we should need much more time than is at our disposal. So in this case, for better understanding, I must give, if not exactly a definition, at least some description of the concept which is to occupy us for some time. Definitions are for the purpose of making clear what is meant when one uses a particular word. In this way, a description of the concept of 'karma' will be given, so that we know what we are talking about when in future the word 'karma' is used in these lectures.

From various previous considerations you will all have formed some idea of what karma is. It is a very abstract idea of karma to call it 'the spiritual law of causes', the law by which certain effects follow certain causes found in spiritual life. This idea of karma is too abstract, because it is on the one hand too narrow and on the other much too comprehensive. If we wish to conceive of karma as a 'law of causes', we must connect it with what is otherwise known in the world as the 'law of causality', the law of cause and effect. Let us be clear about what we understand to be the law of causes in general before we speak of spiritual facts and events.

It is very often emphasized nowadays by natural science that its actual importance lies in the fact that it is founded on the universal law of causes, and that it traces effects to their respective causes. But it is not quite so clear how this linking of cause and effect actually takes place. For you will still find in books of the present day which are held to be scholarly works of philosophy such expressions as the following: an effect is that which follows from a cause. But this is a gross misrepresentation of the facts. In the case of a warm sunbeam falling on a metal plate and making it warmer than before, science would speak of cause and effect in the ordinary sense. But can we claim that the effect – the warming of the metal plate – follows from the cause of the warm sunbeam? If the warm sunbeam had this effect already *within* it, why is it that it warms the metal plate only when it comes into contact with it? Hence, in the world of phenomena, in the *inanimate* world which is all around us, it is necessary, if an effect is to follow a cause, that something should encounter this cause. Unless this takes place one cannot speak of an effect following upon a cause. This preliminary remark, philosophical and abstract though it apparently sounds, is by no means superfluous; for if real progress is to be made in anthroposophical matters we must get into the habit of being extremely accurate in our ideas and not take the casual approach adopted sometimes in other branches of knowledge.

In relation to effects like that of the sunbeam warming a sheet of metal we should not speak of karma at all. Certainly there is causality. The connection between cause and effect is there, but we should never obtain a true idea of karma if we spoke of it only in that way. Hence, we cannot use the term karma in speaking of a simple relation between effect and cause.

Let us now try and develop a more advanced concept of the connection between cause and effect. For instance if we have a bow, and we bend it and shoot off an arrow with it, an effect is caused by the bending of the bow; but we can no more speak of the effect of the shot arrow in connection with its cause as 'karma' than in the foregoing case. But if we consider something else in connection with this process, we shall, to a certain extent, get nearer to the idea of karma, even if we still do not quite grasp it. For example, we may reflect that the bow, if often bent, becomes slack in time. So, from what the bow does and from what happens to it, there will follow not only an effect which shows itself externally, but also one which will react upon the bow itself. Through the frequent bending of the bow something happens to the bow itself. Something which happens through the bending of the bow reacts, so to speak, on the bow. Thus an effect is obtained which reacts on the object by which the effect itself was caused.

This is indeed an important part of the idea of karma. You cannot speak of 'karma' unless an effect is produced which in turn reacts upon the thing or being producing this effect, unless there is this characteristic feature that the effect reacts upon the being who caused it. We thus get somewhat nearer to the idea when it is clear to us that the effects caused by the thing or being must recoil upon that thing or being itself; nevertheless we must not call the slackening of the bow through frequent bending, the 'karma' of the bow, for the following reason. If we have had the bow for three or four weeks and have often bent it so that after this time it becomes slack, then we really have in the slack bow something quite different from the tense bow of four weeks before. Thus when the reacting effect is of such a kind that it makes the thing or the being something quite different, we cannot yet speak of 'karma'. We may speak of karma only when the effects which react upon a being find the same being to react upon, or at any rate that being, in a certain sense, unaltered.

Thus we have come again a little nearer to the idea of karma; but if we describe it in this way we obtain only a very abstract conception of it. If we want to grasp this idea abstractly, we cannot do better than by expressing it in the way we have just done; but one thing more must be added to this idea of karma. If the effect reacts upon the being immediately, that is, if cause and reacting effect are simultaneous, we can hardly speak of karma, for in this case the being from whom the effect proceeded would have actually intended to bring about that result directly. He would, therefore, foresee the effect and would perceive all the elements leading to it. When this is the case we cannot really speak of karma. For instance, we cannot speak of karma in the case of a person performing an act by which he intends to bring about certain results, and who then obtains the desired result in accordance with his purpose. That is to say, between the cause and the effect there must be something hidden from the person when he sets the cause in motion; so that though this connection is really there, it was not actually designed by the person himself. If this connection has not been intended by him then the reason for a connection between cause and effect must be looked for elsewhere than in the intentions of the person in question. That is to say, this reason must be determined by a certain fixed law. Thus karma also includes the fact that the connection between cause and effect is determined by a law independent of whether or not there be direct intention on the part of the being concerned.

We have now grouped together a few principles which may help us to form a clearer picture of what karma is. All of these principles must be part of our concept of karma, and we must not limit ourselves to an abstract definition, or else we shall not be able to comprehend the manifestations of karma in the different spheres of the world. We must now first seek for the manifestations of karma where we first meet with them – in individual human lives.

Can we find anything of the sort in individual lives, and when can we find what we have just presented in our explanation of the concept of karma?

We should find something of the sort if, for example, we experienced something in our life about which we could say: This experience which has come to us is related in a particular way to an earlier experience of ours which we caused ourselves. Let us try in the first place, by mere observation of life, to determine whether this relationship exists. We will take the purely external point of view. Without it we shall never understand the laws by which events and experiences in life are related, any more than someone who has never observed the collision of two billiard balls can understand the elasticity which makes them rebound. Observation of life can lead us to the perception of a law of inter-dependence. Let us take a definite example.

Suppose that a young man in his nineteenth year, who by some accident is obliged to give up a profession which until then had seemed to be marked out for him, and who up to that time had pursued a course of study to prepare him for that profession, through some misfortune to his parents was compelled to give up this profession and, at the age of eighteen, to become a business man. If we observe such incidents in life completely objectively – like one would observe the impact of billiard balls in physics – we might find, for example, that the experience of the business life into which the young man was driven is a stimulating one at first, that he fulfils his duties, learns something and perhaps even makes quite a success out of this career. At the same time one might observe that something very different sets in after a while: a certain malaise, a feeling of discontent. If the change of career took place at eighteen years of age the next few years may pass inconspicuously. Yet, around the twenty-third year, perhaps, it might become apparent that something had taken root in his soul, something quite inexplicable. Looking more closely into the matter, we are likely to find, if the case is not complicated, that the explanation of the boredom arising five years after the change of calling must be sought for in his thirteenth or fourteenth year; for the causes of such a phenomenon are generally to be sought for at about the same period of time before the change of calling as the occurrence we have been describing took place after that change. The man in question when he was a schoolboy of thirteen, five years before the change of vocation, might have experienced something in his soul which gave him a feeling of inner happiness. Supposing that no change of profession had taken place, then that to which the youth had accustomed himself in his thirteenth year would have been fulfilled in later life and would have borne fruit. Then, however, came the change which at first interested the young man and engaged his soul; something entered his soul-life which repressed what had occupied it before. It is possible to repress something for a certain time, but through the very fact of being repressed it gains a special force, especially inwardly; an elastic force, as it were, is built up in the soul. This might be compared with the squeezing of an india-rubber ball which we can compress to a certain point where it resists, and if it were allowed to spring back it would do so in proportion to the force with which we have just compressed it.

In like manner experiences like the one just described – what the young man experienced in his soul in his thirteenth year had consolidated by the time the change of career came along – can also be repressed in a certain way; but then, after a while, resistance arises in the soul. Then one can see how this resistance grows to finally show its effect. Because the soul lacks something it would have if the change of career had not taken place, that which had been repressed emerges and manifests as discontent and boredom with life.

So this is a case where the person concerned experienced something, did something in his thirteenth, fourteenth year, and did something else later, i.e. changed his career; and we can see how these causes show their effect later on, by reacting upon the same person. In a case like this we should have to apply the concept of karma to an individual human life. Now one ought not to object: But we have known of cases where nothing of the kind was shown! That may well be. Yet it would not occur to a physicist examining the laws of velocity of a falling stone to say that the law would not be valid if the stone was deflected by a blow. We need to learn to observe properly and exclude all phenomena which do not affect the establishing of the law concerned. Surely such an individual who, if nothing else intervened, experiences the effects of impressions in his thirteenth year in the form of boredom in his twenty-third year, would not experience this particular boredom if he had married in the meantime, for example. But such an occurrence has no bearing on the establishment of the fundamental law. What is important is that we find the right factors which will lead us to a particular law. Observation in itself is nothing, only methodical observation will enable us to understand the law. For the study of the law of karma we must apply such methodical observation in the right way.

Now let us assume – for the purpose of establishing the karma of a particular individual – that this person suffered a heavy blow of destiny in his twenty-fifth year; this event caused him pain and suffering. If we confine our observations to simply stating that this heavy blow of destiny broke in upon this life and filled it with pain and suffering, in other words, if we do not go beyond the mere observation, we shall never understand karmic connections. But if we go further and examine the life of such an individual who in his twenty-fifth year experienced that stroke of destiny, in his fiftieth year we might arrive at a view such as this one: the person we are looking at has developed into a virtuous and hard-working individual, well established in life; now we look back over his life and we find that at the age of twenty he was still a good-for-nothing, with no initiative at all. Then, at the age of twenty-five, a severe blow of destiny hit him. If this blow had not hit him – we may now say – he would have remained a good-for-nothing character. In other words, the heavy blow of destiny was the cause of the virtue and competence manifest in the individual's fiftieth year.

Such facts also teach us that we should be mistaken if we considered the blow of destiny in the twenty-fifth year as mere effect. For if we ask ourselves what the stroke of destiny caused, we must go beyond mere observation. But if we consider the blow not as an effect at the end of the phenomena which preceded it, but place it rather at the beginning of the subsequent events, and consider it as a cause, we will find that even our feelings in relation to this blow of destiny may change substantially. We shall very likely be grieved if we think of it only as an effect, but if we think of it as the cause of what happens later on, we shall probably be glad and feel pleasure over it. For we can say that thanks to the fateful blow the man who experienced it has become a decent human being.

So we see that our attitude is essentially different in so far as we consider an event in life as cause or as effect. It matters a great deal whether we consider what happens in life as mere effect or as cause. It is true that if we start our investigations at the time of the painful event, we cannot then clearly perceive the direct effect, but if we have arrived at the law of karma by the observation of similar cases, that law can itself say to us: An event is painful perhaps now because it appears to us merely as the result of what has happened previously, but it can also be looked upon as the starting point of what is to follow. Then we can foresee the blow of fate as the starting point and the cause of the results, and this places the matter in quite a different light. Thus the law of karma itself may be a source of consolation if we accustom ourselves to set an event not only at the end, but at the beginning of a series of events. It is important that we learn to study life methodically, and to place things in the right relationship to one another as cause and effect. If we carry out these observations thoroughly, we shall notice events in the life of a person which take place with a certain regularity; others, again, appear quite irregularly in the same life. In this way you will be able to discover remarkable connections in human life, provided that you observe it properly, and this involves looking further than the end of your nose. Unfortunately the phenomena of human life are only observed over short spans of time at present, no more than a few years at most; and people are not in a habit of relating what happened after many years to earlier events which might well have caused the later. That is why there are very few people today capable of establishing a certain connection between the beginning and the end of human life. Yet this connection is extraordinarily instructive.

Supposing we have brought up a child during the first seven years of his life without ever assuming – as it is generally assumed – that if an individual is to lead a good and useful life he must conform to our own standards of what makes a person good and useful. For in that case we would be keen to train the child strictly in everything we consider essential to being good and useful. Whereas if we recognize at the outset that one can be good and useful in many different ways, and that there is no need to determine in which of these ways the child with his individual talents is to become a good and useful human being, we would say: 'Whatever may be my ideas of a good and useful person, this child is to become one through having his best talents brought out, and these I must first discover. What matter the rules by which I myself feel bound? The child himself must feel the need to do what he does. If I wish to develop the child according to his individual talents, I must try first to develop tendencies latent in him and draw them out, so that he may above all realize them and act in accordance with them. This shows us that there are two quite different ways of influencing a child in the first seven years of his life.'

If we now look at the child in his later life it will be a long time before the essential effects are manifested of what we have in this way brought into the first years of his life. Observation of life reveals to us that the actual effects of what was put into the child's soul in his earliest years as causes do not manifest until the very evening of life. A person may possess to the very end of his life an active mind, if he has been, as a child, educated in this way; that is, if the living, inherent tendencies of his soul have been observed and naturally developed. If we have drawn out and developed his innate powers we shall see the fruits in the evening of his life displayed as a rich soul-life. On the other hand, in a starved and impoverished soul and a correspondingly weak old age (for we shall see later on how a starved soul reacts on the body), is manifested what we have done wrong in our treatment of a person in earliest childhood. This is something in human life which in a certain way is so regular that it is applicable to everyone as a connection between cause and effect.

The same connection may also be found in the intermediate stages of life, and I will deal with this in due course. The way in which we treat a child from his seventh to his fourteenth year produces effects in that part of his life which precedes the final stage, and thus we see cause and effect working in cycles. What existed as cause in the earliest years comes out as effect in the latest ones. But in addition to these causes and effects in individual lives which run their course in cycles, there is what may be described as a straight line law.

In our example which showed how the thirteenth year influenced the twenty-third, we see how cause and effect are so connected with human life that what a person has experienced leads to after-effects which in their turn react upon him. Thus karma is fulfilled in individual lives. However, if we only search for the connection between causes and effects in one life of a particular human being, we shall not arrive at an explanation of human life in general. We will develop this thought further in the next few sessions. I am only pointing out something you are already familiar with from the teachings of spiritual science: that human life between birth and death is the repetition of earlier human lives.

If we now seek for the chief characteristic of the life between birth and death, we can describe this as being the extension of one and the same consciousness – essentially at least – throughout the entire period between birth and death. If you call to mind the earliest parts of your life, you will say: There is indeed, a point of time when my recollections of life begin, which does not coincide with my birth, but which comes somewhat later. With the exception of initiates this is how people experience this – they refer to their consciousness as reaching back to just that point. There is, indeed, something very remarkable in the period of time between birth and the beginning of this recollection of life, and we shall return to it again as it will throw light upon important matters. Except, then, for this period between birth and the beginning of memory we can say that life between birth and death is characterized by the fact of one consciousness extending throughout that period of time.

Normally people do not look for the causes of what happened to them later in life in earlier periods of their life; yet it would be possible to find such connections if sufficient attention were paid and if all possible aspects were properly investigated. When we use the consciousness we all have in the form of our memory consciousness and try to place before our soul the connection between earlier and later events in the karmic sense, we might say, for example: I can see that certain things that have happened to me might not have happened if this or that event had not taken place earlier in my life. Or else: Now I am paying for what my early upbringing has done to me. Even if all you achieve is understanding a certain connection between the wrong others have caused in you through the way you were brought up and certain events in your later life, it will be helpful to an extent. It is easier then to find ways and means of counteracting the early harm suffered. Indeed, recognizing such connections between causes and effects in the different periods of our life which we can contemplate with our ordinary consciousness can be of very great benefit. For if we attain such knowledge we may accomplish something else, too. Naturally, when someone at the age of eighty looks back over his life to find the causes of events in his eightieth year in his earliest childhood, he may find it difficult to find ways of compensating for what he suffered then, and even if he did go about it in the right manner it would not help him a great deal. But if he takes the right approach before, and looks back in, say, his fortieth year on the wrongs that have been done to him, he might then have time to take measures against them.

Thus we see that it is desirable to reach beyond our immediate life karma and attain to an understanding of the laws of karma. This may be very useful in our life. What should a person do who in his fortieth year attempts to avert the effect of wrongs done to him, or wrongs which he himself did in his twelfth year? He will do everything to avert the consequences of his own misdeeds or those of others towards him. He will to a certain extent replace by another the effect which would inevitably have arisen had he not intervened. The knowledge of what happened in his twelfth year will lead him to a definite action in his fortieth year, which he would not have taken unless he had known what it was that had happened in his twelfth year. What, then, has the man done by looking back at his early life? He has applied his consciousness to make a certain effect follow a certain cause. He has willed the effect and has brought it about. This shows us how, in the line of karmic consequences, our will can intervene and bring about something which takes the place of the karmic effects which would otherwise have followed. If we consider such a case in which a person has quite consciously brought about a connection between cause and effect in life, we could conclude that in this case karma, or the laws of karma, have penetrated his consciousness, and he has himself, in a certain way, brought about the karmic effect.

Let us now apply what we know about the repeated earth lives of a human being to such a picture. The consciousness of which we have just spoken which extends, with the exception mentioned, throughout the period between birth and death, is due to the fact that the human being is able to use his brain as an instrument. When we pass through the gate of death a different sort of consciousness comes into play – one that is independent of the brain and works under completely different conditions. We also know that this consciousness which extends up to the point of our next birth experiences a sort of review of everything we have done in our life between our last birth and death. In this period between birth and death we must first form the intention to look back at any wrongs which have been done to us, or which we have done, if we wish to counteract these wrongs karmically. After death, in looking back over life, we see what we have done wrong or otherwise; and at the same time we see how these deeds have affected us; we see how a certain deed of ours has improved or debased us. If we have brought suffering to anyone, we have sunk and become of less value; we are less perfect, so to speak. Now, if we look back after death we see numerous events of the sort, and we say to ourselves: through this I have become less perfect. Then, in the consciousness after death, the will and power arise to win back, when the opportunities occur, the value we have lost; the will, that is to say, to make compensation for every wrong committed. Thus between death and a new birth the tendency and intention is formed to make good what has been done wrong, in order to regain the state of perfection appropriate to the human being which has been compromised by the respective deed.

Then we return once more to life on earth. Our consciousness changes again. We do not recollect the time between death and rebirth, or the resolutions to make compensation. But the intention remains within us and although we do not know that we must do such and such a thing to compensate for such and such an act, yet we are impelled by the power within us to make the compensation. We can form an idea of what happens when someone in his twentieth year encounters some great suffering. With the consciousness he possesses between birth and death, he will be dejected by his suffering; but if he could remember his resolutions made between death and a new birth, he would also be able to feel the power which drove him into the position where he was able to encounter this suffering because he felt that only by passing through it would he win back the degree of perfection which he has lost and was now to regain. When, therefore, the ordinary consciousness says: 'The trial is there, and you are suffering from it,' it sees only the trouble itself, and not the effect it produces; but the other consciousness which can look back upon all the time between death and a new birth sees the intentional seeking for the suffering or other misfortune.

This is indeed what we find when we look at human life from a higher point of view. Then we can see that fateful events occur in human life which are not the results of causes in the individual life itself, but are the effects of causes perceived in another state of consciousness, namely, the consciousness we had before our birth. If we grasp these ideas thoroughly, we shall see that in the first place we have a consciousness which extends over the time between birth and death, which we call the consciousness of the individual person. And then we see that there is a consciousness which works beyond birth and death of which man in his ordinary consciousness knows nothing, but which nevertheless works in the same way as the ordinary consciousness. We have, therefore, shown first of all how someone may take on his own karma, and in his fortieth year make some compensation so that the causes of his twelfth year may not come to effect. This is a way of taking karma into one's individual personal consciousness. In the case, however, where someone is driven to suffer pain in order to compensate for something and to become a better human being, this also proceeds from the person himself; not from his personal consciousness, but from a more comprehensive consciousness which encompasses the time between death and a new birth. That being in us which is encompassed by this later consciousness we will call the 'individuality', and the consciousness which is being continually interrupted by the personal consciousness, we will call the 'individual consciousness'. Thus we see karma working in relation to the individual human being.

In spite of this, we shall not understand human life if we only follow the sequence of phenomena as we have just done, if we only fix our attention on the causes that lie within us and the effects we seek as a result, all of which concern our own individual being. We need only bring forward a simple case to make things clearer, and we shall at once see that we cannot understand human life if we take into consideration only what has already been said. Let us take a discoverer or an inventor, Columbus,[1] for example, or the inventor of the steam-engine,[2] or any others: in the discovery there is a distinct action, a distinct achievement. If we examine the action and seek for the cause why the person did it, we shall always find such causes by searching along the lines just pointed out. We shall find in his individual and personal karma the reasons why Columbus sailed to America and why he determined to do so at just that particular time. But now we might ask if the cause must be sought for only in his personal and individual karma; and is the action only to be considered as an effect for the individuality working in Columbus. That Columbus discovered America had certain consequences for him. He rose by doing so, and became more perfect, and this will show itself in the development of his individuality in succeeding lives. But what effects has this achievement had on other people? Must it not also be considered as a cause which affected the lives of countless human beings?

This, again, is still rather an abstract consideration of such a question which we can grasp much more deeply by looking at human life over long periods of time. Let us consider human life in the Egyptian-Chaldean age which preceded the Græco-Latin. If we examine this age in relation to what it imparted to human beings and what they experienced at that time, we shall find something very peculiar. If we compare this epoch with our own, we shall perceive that what is happening in our own time is connected with what happened in the Egyptian-Chaldean civilization. The Græco-Latin lies between the two. In our time certain things would not happen unless other things had happened in the Egyptian-Chaldean times. The scientific achievements of today are equally derived from powers which have developed in the human soul. However, the human souls who worked in our time were also incarnated in the Egyptian-Chaldean age, and at that time they underwent certain experiences without which they would not be able to accomplish what they do today. If the pupils of the ancient Egyptian temple priests had not learned in Egyptian astrology about the relations existing between the heavenly bodies, they would not later on have been able to penetrate into the secrets of the world, nor would certain souls in the present age have possessed the abilities to explore the regions of the heavens. For instance, how did Kepler arrive at his discoveries?[3] He did so because within him there was a soul who in the Egyptian-Chaldean epoch had acquired the forces necessary for the discoveries which he was to make in the fifth epoch. It fills us with inner satisfaction to see in certain souls memories arising, as it were, that the seeds of their present deeds were laid in the past. Kepler, one of the men who has played a most important part in the investigation of the laws of the universe, said of himself:

'Yes, it is I who have robbed the golden vessels of the Egyptians to make an offering to my God far removed from Egyptian bounds. If you will forgive me, I will rejoice, but if you blame me I must bear it; here I throw the dice and I write this book. What matter if it is read today or later – even if centuries must elapse before it is read! God himself had to wait six thousand years for the one who recognized his work.'[4]

Here we have a sporadic memory rising in Kepler of what he received as a germ for the work which he, in his personal life as Kepler, accomplished. Hundreds of similar cases might be given. But we see in Kepler something more than the mere manifestation of effects which were the result of causes in a previous incarnation – we see a manifestation which has its significance for the whole of mankind – a manifestation of something which was equally important for humanity in a previous epoch. We see how a person is placed in a special position in order to do something for the whole of mankind. We see that, not only in individual lives but in the whole of humanity, there are connections between cause and effect which stretch over wide periods of time, and we can deduce that the karmic law of the individual will intersect what we may call the karmic laws of humanity. Sometimes intersections of this kind are difficult to trace. Imagine what would have happened to our astronomy if the telescope had not been discovered at that particular time.[5] If we look back at the history of the telescope we see how tremendously important the discovery has been. Now it is well known that the discovery of the telescope was made in the following way. Some children were playing with lenses in an optician's workshop and by chance, as one might say, they had so placed the optical lenses that someone hit upon the idea of employing this arrangement to make something like a tele-scope. Think how deeply you must search in order to arrive at the individual karma of the children and the karma of humanity which led to the discovery at that particular mo-ment. Try to think the two facts out together, and you will see in what a remarkable manner the karma of single individuals and the karma of the whole of humanity intersect and weave into each other. You must admit that the whole of the development of mankind would have been different if such and such a thing had not come to pass when it did.

To ask such a question as: 'What would have happened to the Roman Empire if the Greeks had not beaten off the Persian attack in the Persian wars at a particular time?' is often quite futile, but to ask: 'How did it happen that the Persian war ended in this way?' is by no means futile. If we follow up this question and seek an answer we shall see that in the East certain achievements only came about because there were despotic rulers who were totally self-seeking and who, to gain their ends, joined forces with the sacrificial priests. The whole organization of the eastern state was at that time necessary for any given thing to be accomplished, and this arrangement brought with it all the trouble which resulted in the Greeks – a differently constituted people – defeating the eastern attack at a critical moment. How, then, must we consider the karma of those who worked in Greece to resist the Persian attack? We shall find much that is personal in the karma of those in question, but we shall also find that their personal karma is linked with the karma of nations and of humanity, so that we are justified in saying that the karma of humanity placed these particular persons in that particular place at that time. We see here the karma of humanity affecting the individual karma, and we must ask how these things are interwoven. But we may go still further and consider yet another connection.

We can look back to a time in the evolution of our earth when there was as yet no mineral kingdom. The evolution of the earth was preceded by the Saturn, Sun and Moon evolutions, where as yet there was no mineral kingdom in our sense of the word. It was on this earth that our minerals first took on their present forms. But because the mineral kingdom became separated in the course of the earth's evolution, it will remain a separate kingdom to the end. Before that, human beings, animals and plants had developed without the mineral kingdom. In order that later the other kingdoms might make further progress, they had to separate the mineral kingdom out of themselves; but after they had done this, they could only develop on a planet which had a firm mineral form. They could have developed in no other way than this, if we admit that the formation of a mineral kingdom took place in the way we have said. The mineral kingdom is there, and the subsequent fate of the other kingdoms depends on the existence of this mineral kingdom which was formed within our earth in remote ages of antiquity. So something happened connected with the fact of the formation of the mineral kingdom which must be taken into account in all the later evolutions of the earth. What follows as the result of the formation of the mineral kingdom finds its fulfilment in everything that comes into existence. Once again, what happened earlier will be karmically fulfilled in subsequent ages. On the earth is fulfilled what was prepared on the earth long ago. There is a connection between what happened earlier and what came to pass later but this is also a connection which in its effects reacts upon the being which caused it. Human beings, animals and plants have separated from the mineral kingdom, and the latter reacts upon them! Thus we see that it is possible to speak of the karma of the earth.

Finally, we can bring to light something, the elements of which we can find in the general principles described in my book, *Occult Science*.[6] We know that certain beings remained behind at the stage of the old Moon evolution and that these beings did so for the purpose of giving to human beings certain definite qualities. Not only beings but also substances remained from the old Moon-time of the earth. At the Moon stage there remained behind beings who influenced our earth's existence as luciferic beings.[7] As a result of this, certain effects are manifested on our earth of which the causes are to be found in the Moon life. But from the point of being of actual substance something analogous was also brought about. As we now see our solar system, we find it composed of heavenly bodies which regularly carry out recurrent movements which display a certain inner completeness. But we find other heavenly bodies which move, indeed, with a certain rhythm, but break through, as it were, the usual laws of the solar system. These are the comets. Now, the substance of a comet does not obey the laws which exist in our solar system, but such laws as prevailed in the old Moon-existence. Indeed, the laws of that old Moon are preserved in the life of the comet. I have already often pointed out that spiritual science had provided evidence for these laws before they were confirmed by natural science. In Paris, in 1906, I drew attention to the fact that, during the old Moon existence, certain combinations of carbon and nitrogen played a similar part to that played at the present day on our earth by combinations of oxygen and carbon, carbon monoxide, carbon dioxide, and so on.[8] These latter have something deadly in them. Cyanide combinations, prussic acid combinations, played a similar part during the old Moon-existence. This was pointed out by spiritual science in 1906, and in other lectures it was shown that comets bring the laws of the old Moon-existence into our solar system, so that not only the luciferic beings remained behind, but also the laws of the old Moon-substance, which work in our solar system in an irregular way. We have always said that a comet must contain something like cyanide compounds in its atmosphere. Only much later, namely this year, 1910, was prussic acid found by spectrum analysis in the comet, proving what had already been made known by spiritual science.[9]

You may turn to this for evidence when people say: Show us for once how one might actually discover something by means of spiritual science! There are other phenomena of this nature, if people would only observe them. So there is something of the old Moon-existence working in our present earth existence.

Now we come to the question: Can it be maintained that something spiritual lies behind a phenomenon observed by means of the outer senses?

To one who knows spiritual science it is quite clear that there is something spiritual behind all material realities. When something relating to substance works into our earth existence from the Old Moon existence, when a comet shines upon our earth, there is also something spiritual working behind it. We can even distinguish what spiritual force is working in the case of Halley's comet.[10] Halley's comet is the outward expression of a new impulse of materialism every time it comes within the sphere of our earth's existence. To the world of the present day this may seem superstitious, but people should remember how they themselves relate spiritual influences to the constellations. Who would deny that an Eskimo is a different sort of human being from a Hindu, because in the polar regions the sun's rays strike the earth at a different angle! Everywhere the scientists themselves relate spiritual effects on mankind to constellations. A spiritual impulse towards materialism is coincident with the appearance of Halley's comet and there is evidence of this impulse. The appearance of this comet in 1835 was followed by that materialistic culture of the second half of the nineteenth century, and its appearance before that was followed by the materialistic enlightenment campaign of the French Encyclopædists. That is the connection. In order that certain things may enter into the earth's existence, the causes must be laid long before outside the earth; this is in fact a case of world karma. After all, why was spiritual and material substance driven out from the old Moon? In order that certain effects could react on the beings that caused this. The luciferic beings were separated off and had to develop in a different way, so that for the beings on earth free will and the possibilities of evil could originate. Here we have something which in its karmic effect extends beyond our earth existence; here is a glimpse of world karma.

We have now dealt with the conception of karma, its significance for each personality, each individuality, and for all mankind. We have described its influence within our earth and beyond it, and we have found something else which we may describe as world karma.

Thus we find the karmic law of connection between cause and effect which works in such a way that the effect in its turn works back upon the cause; and yet in reacting it keeps its essence and remains the same. We find this law of karma ruling everywhere in the world in so far as we recognize the world as spiritual in origin. We dimly sense karma revealing itself in so many different ways, in entirely different spheres, and we feel how the different branches of karma – personal karma, the karma of humanity, earth karma, world karma, and so on, will intersect each other. And we know that this is the key to understanding life, for life can only be understood in its details if we can find how the various karmic influences are interwoven.

LECTURE 2

Karma and the Animal Kingdom

Hamburg, 17 May 1910

Before we come to the question of human karma, a number of preliminary considerations are necessary. Yesterday I gave you a kind of description of the concept of karma, and today I shall have to say something about karma and the animal kingdom.

In the course of this cycle of lectures I shall discuss what might be called external evidence of the reality of karmic laws whenever there is a good reason to point specially to such external evidence. You will find that through this you will acquire the ability to speak about karma and its underlying reason to other people who may raise one question or another about it, or doubt the concept of karma as a whole. But let us first develop the background to this.

What is more natural than to ask how animal life and animal fate are related to what we call the course of human karma? This encompasses after all the most important and incisive questions of man's destiny.

The relation of man on the earth to the animal kingdom differs with the various epochs and also with the various peoples. It is certainly not without interest to see that in the case of the peoples who have preserved the best parts of the ancient sacred wisdom of humanity there is a deeply sympathetic and loving treatment of animals. For example, in the Buddhist world which has preserved important parts of the old conceptions of the world held by mankind in ancient times, we find a very sympathetic treatment of animals, a treatment and a feeling towards the animal kingdom which many people in Europe cannot yet understand.

You will find it among other peoples, too; especially where a nation has preserved some of the ancient inherited wisdom in one place or another, you will find a kind of friendship, something approaching a human treatment of animals. An example is the Arab and his treatment of his horse.

In contrast to this it can hardly be denied that in those parts of the world where a kind of world-view of the future is being prepared, in the western countries, there is little understanding for such sympathetic attitudes towards the animal kingdom. And it is also remarkable that the idea of the animal as a non-sentient being with no special soul-life, the idea of the animal as a kind of automaton, should have emerged in the course of the Middle Ages right until our day in those very countries where the Christian world-view was spreading. And it has been pointed out – perhaps not without reason, if not always with great understanding – that this idea advanced by a great body of western philosophy, that animals are automatons and possess no actual soul, has trickled down into those parts of the population where there is no compassion for the animal and where there is often no limit, either, to the cruelty meted out to animals. Indeed, things have reached a point where the thoughts of a great philosopher of modern times, Descartes, about the animal kingdom, have been thoroughly misunderstood.[1]

Of course, we must clearly understand that the idea of animals as mere automata has never been put forward by any of the really eminent souls of western culture; neither did Descartes hold this view, although in many books on philosophy you may read that he did so. But that is not true.

It is true that he does not ascribe to the animal a soul which is able to develop to where it can prove, for instance, the existence of God out of its own consciousness of self; nevertheless, he does say that the animal is permeated and animated by the so-called Spirits of Life which, though they do not present such a complete individuality as the 'I' of man, do nevertheless work as soul in the animal organization. It is indeed characteristic that one should have been able to misunderstand Descartes so completely, for this shows us that in past centuries there has been the tendency in our western development to ascribe to the animal something merely automatic. We should not have misunderstood this had we gone to work conscientiously, but we have read it into Descartes. It is the characteristic of western civilization that it had to be developed out of the elements of materialism; one may even say that the dawn of Christianity took place in such a way that this important impulse in human evolution was first planted into a materialistic western mentality. The materialism of modern times is only a consequence of the fact that even the most spiritual of religions, Christianity, was at first conceived of in purely materialistic terms in the West. It is, after all, the destiny of western humanity, of the western nations, that they have to work their way up from the low grounds of materialism and develop – through overcoming these materialistic views and tendencies – the forces which will lead to the highest spiritual life. It is a consequence of this destiny, this karma, that the peoples of the West have a tendency to consider animals as mere automata. Those who cannot penetrate into the working of spiritual life and can only judge by what surrounds them in the external world of the senses, would, from the impressions of that world, easily arrive at an idea about the animal kingdom which places the animals on the lowest scale. On the other hand, conceptions of the world which still contain elements of the primordial spiritual truths, the ancient wisdom of humanity, preserved a kind of knowledge of what exists spiritually in the animal kingdom; and in spite of all misunderstanding, in spite of all that has crept into their views of the world and destroyed their purity, they have not been able to forget that spiritual activities and spiritual laws are active in the life and development of the animal kingdom.

Thus, if on the one hand, because of our lack of spiritual conceptions, we are compelled to admit ignorance concerning the animal soul nature, we must not on the other hand deceive ourselves by applying directly to the animal kingdom that idea of karma which helps to understand human destiny and human karma; for this would be the result of a purely materialistic conception of the world. This must not be done. I have already pointed out yesterday that it is essential to consider the idea of karma with exactitude. We should go astray if we sought in the animal kingdom for instances of the recoil of an action on the being from which the cause has proceeded. We can only comprehend the vast ramifications of karmic law if we go beyond a single human life between birth and death, and follow man through his consecutive reincarnations; then we shall find that the recoil of a cause which we have set in motion in one life can only come into action in a later one. The regular law of karma stretches from life to life, and the effects of causes need not operate – indeed, when we consider karma on the whole, quite certainly do not operate – in the same life between birth and death.

From the more elementary teachings of spiritual science we already know that in the case of animals we cannot speak of a reincarnation such as takes place with man. In the animal kingdom we find nothing resembling that human individuality which is preserved when a person passes through the gate of death and lives a particular life in the spiritual world during the period from death to a new birth in order then to enter existence again by a new birth. We cannot conceive of animal death in the same way as we conceive of human death, for all that we describe as the destiny of the human individuality after a person has passed through the gate of death is not the same in the animal kingdom. And if we were to believe that in an individual animal which we have before us we could look for the reincarnated being of an animal which had previously existed on the earth – as we can do in the case of man – we should be entirely wrong. Today there is a general tendency to view the phenomena of life superficially, with no regard to their inner nature; hence the really great opposites, the fundamental differences between man and animal, are simply not perceived. From a purely materialistic point of view the outward phenomenon of death seems to be the same in man as in the animal. So one may easily believe, when observing the life of an animal between its birth and death, that the various phenomena in the individual life of the animal are comparable with those in the personal life of a human being between birth and death. But this would be quite wrong. That is why I would like to point out some of the essential differences between animal and man.

To understand fully this fundamental difference between the animal and the human being we need to take an objective view of what our senses reveal to us and relate this to the fruits of our thinking. We find a phenomenon to which attention is also drawn by scientists; however, they don't quite know what to make of it – namely, the phenomenon that man has really to learn the simplest things. In the course of his history man has had to learn the use of the most primitive tools, and our children still have to learn the simplest things, and have to spend a certain time in order to learn them. Man has to make efforts to produce even the simplest things, or to manufacture his instruments and tools. When, on the other hand, we observe the animals we are obliged to admit how much easier it is for them in this respect. Think how the beaver builds its complicated dwelling. It does not need to learn; it knows how to do it, because it brings the knowledge with it as an inherent law, just as we human beings bring with us the 'art' of changing our teeth at about seven years of age. No one needs to learn that. In the same way, animals such as the beavers bring with them the capability to build their houses. If you observe the animal kingdom you will find that the animals bring with them definite capacities by which they can achieve things which human art, great as it is, is far from achieving.

The question may now arise: How does it come about that when a human being is born he is less capable than, for example, a hen, or a beaver; and that he has first, with great pains, to acquire what these creatures already bring with them? This is a very important question. And we need above all to develop a sense, or feeling, for the importance of this question. For it is much more relevant to our view of the world that we should be able to put the right question than that we should acquire masses of knowledge. Facts may be right, but they need not always be essential to our world-view. Although we shall today go into the causes of these phenomena from the standpoint of spiritual science, it would carry us too far if we were to show in detail why this is so. But I will refer to it in a few words.

If with the aid of spiritual science we go back into human evolution in the primeval past we shall find that the forces which are at the disposal of the beaver or any other animal, in order that they should bring such artistic powers into the world, were at one time at the disposal of human beings. It is not that man in a primordial past missed this endowment of capabilities while the animals took them all for themselves; he also received these powers, indeed in a far greater degree than the animals. For although the latter bring a certain great artistic skill into the world with them, this is, however, limited in extent. Fundamentally at birth the human being can do nothing at all, and he has first to learn everything which concerns the outer world. This is somewhat strongly expressed, but you will understand what I mean. When a human being learns, it is soon shown that he can become many-sided, and that as regards the development of certain artistic capacities, as well as others, this can be far richer than that of an animal. So the human being originally brought with him more abundant powers, which he does not bring today. The peculiar phenomenon comes to light, that originally man and animal were similarly endowed; and if we were to go back to the old Saturn evolution, we should find that there was absolutely no difference between human and animal development. All these capabilities were common to both. What then has happened in the meantime, that the animal now brings with it into existence all sorts of capacities, while human beings are really clumsy when they come into the world? How has man behaved in the meantime that he now no longer possesses all he once brought with him? Has he foolishly wasted it in the course of evolution, while the animals have preserved it like thrifty housekeepers? These are perfectly legitimate questions.

Man has not wasted these powers which today the animals manifest as external capacities; he has only transformed them, but into something which differs from what the animals possess. They have applied them to external works;

beavers build their homes and wasps their nests, but man has transformed and incorporated within himself the same forces which the animals manifest outwardly, and by this means he has brought into being what we call his higher human organization. In order that human beings should be able to walk upright, in order that they should have a more perfect brain, and, in general, a more perfect inner organization, certain forces were necessary, and these are the same forces with which the beaver constructs his dwelling. The beaver builds his home, but the human being has turned the forces inwards upon himself, to his brain, etc., and so he has nothing left over with which to work outwardly. So if we, at the present time, move among the animals with a more perfect constitution, it is due to the fact that we have applied inwardly all the forces that the beaver expends in an outward way. We have our beaver-building within us, and therefore we are no longer able to manifest these forces outwardly in the same way. When we take a comprehensive view of the world, we understand the origin of the various capacities which exist in creation, and how they appear to us today.

Why had man to turn towards an inner organization the special forces which we see manifested in the external achievements of animals? Because only by acquiring this inner organization could man become the vehicle of what at the present time is the 'I' which progresses from incarnation to incarnation. No other organization could have become this bearer of the 'I', because it depends altogether upon the external shrine whether an 'I'-individuality is able to be active in the earthly existence or not. It could not do so if the external organization were not suited to the 'I'-individuality. Everything contributed to making this organization thus suitable, and to this end a particular arrangement had to be made, the essentials of which we already know.

We know that the Moon evolution preceded the Earth evolution.[2] Before that again was the Sun evolution which was preceded by a Saturn evolution. When the ancient Moon evolution came to an end, man was at a stage of development – as regards his external life – which may be described as animal-humanity. At that time this external human organization had not progressed far enough for it to become the vehicle of an 'I'-individuality. It was the Earth evolution of man which had the task of embodying the 'I' in this organization. But this could only come about by regulating our Earth evolution in a very special way. When the old Moon development came to an end, everything dissolved, so to speak, into chaos. After an appropriate period of cosmic twilight, the new cosmos of our Earth evolution came forth. In it was contained everything which, as our solar system, is connected with us and the Earth. From this whole, from this cosmic unity there split off all the other planetary bodies belonging to our special Earth existence. We need not go into the manner in which the other planets, Jupiter, Mars, etc., split off. We have only to point out that at a certain period of our Earth-phase of evolution, our Earth and our Sun separated. While the Sun had already separated and was sending down its activities to the Earth from outside, our Earth was still united with the present Moon, so that the substances and spiritual forces which at the present day belong to the Moon, at that time were still united with the Earth.

We have often touched upon the question as to what would have happened if the Sun had not split away from the Earth, and passed over into that condition in which it works on the Earth from outside as it does now. In the beginning, when the Earth was still united to the Sun, the conditions were quite different and the whole cosmic system included the ancestors of the human organization, making one unity. It is absurd to look at modern conditions and say: What nonsense those anthroposophists talk! If that had been so, all beings would have been burnt up! But these beings were so organized that at that time they could exist under conditions quite different from those of this epoch. If the Sun had remained in union with the Earth, forces very different and much more violent would have remained with the Earth; and the consequence would have been that the whole evolution of the Earth would have progressed with such violence and speed that it would have been impossible for the human organization to develop as it should. Therefore it was necessary that the Earth should be given a slower tempo, and denser forces placed at its disposal. This could only be brought about by the withdrawal of the violent and stormy forces from the Earth. The forces of the Sun worked less violently when acting from outside after withdrawal from the Earth. Through this, however, something else took place. The Earth was now in a condition in which mankind could again not progress in the right way. The state of the Earth was now too dense, and it exercised a drying and petrifying action on all life. If conditions had remained so, man would have again been unable to develop. This was remedied by a special arrangement. Some time after the exit of the Sun the present Moon left the Earth, and took away the retarding forces which would have brought all life to a slow death. Thus the Earth remained behind between Sun and Moon, selecting exactly the right tempo for the human organization, enabling it to take up an 'I' and to be the bearer of the individuality which goes on from incarnation to incarnation. The human organization as it exists today was produced from the cosmos under no other conditions than through this process – first the separation of the Sun and then that of the Moon.

Someone might perhaps say: If I had been the Almighty I would have done it differently; I would very soon have produced such a combination that the human organization would have been able to progress in the manner it had to progress! Why was it necessary that first the Sun had to withdraw and then after a time the Moon?

The person who thinks in this way thinks much too abstractly. He does not reflect that when, in the universal order, so complex a thing as the human organization is to be produced, a special arrangement is necessary for each single part. One cannot convert into reality what human thought invents and imagines. Abstractly one can think anything, but in true spiritual science one has to learn to think concretely so that one says: The human organization is not a simple thing; it consists of a physical body, an etheric body and an astral body. These three parts had first to be brought into a particular equilibrium, so that the several parts should be correctly related to one another. This could only take place through this threefold process: first, the formation of the unitary cosmos – the entire cosmic unity of Earth, Sun and Moon together. Then something had to be done that would work in a retarding way on the human etheric body which would otherwise have consumed all evolution too fiercely – this was accomplished by the withdrawal of the Sun. Then again the Moon had to be withdrawn, because otherwise, through the astral body, the human organization would have died. These three processes had to take place because of the human being's threefold organization.

Thus we see that we owe our existence and our present qualities to a complicated arrangement in the cosmos. But we also know that the evolutions of all the kingdoms of nature do not by any means proceed at the same rate as the general evolution. From various lectures given in preceding years, we know that during each of the planetary incarnations of the earth certain beings have always remained behind the general evolution. Then, as evolution proceeds, they live in conditions which do not fully correspond to this evolution. We also know that fundamentally all evolution can only proceed in the right way through the remaining behind of these entities. During the old Moon evolution certain beings remained behind as the luciferic beings, and through them much that is evil has resulted; but to them we also owe what makes human existence possible, namely, the possibility of freedom, of the free development of our inner being. Indeed, we may say that in a certain sense the remaining behind of the luciferic beings was a sacrifice. They remained behind so that during the Earth existence they would exercise certain activities; they could bestow on man the qualities which pertain to his dignity and self-determination. We must accustom ourselves to entirely different ideas from those which are customary; for according to the usual ideas one might perhaps say that the luciferic spirits failed to progress and had to remain behind; and we could not excuse their negligence. But it was not a question of the negligence of the luciferic beings; in a certain sense their remaining behind was a sacrifice, in order that they might be able to work on our earthy humanity through what they acquired by this sacrifice.

From the last lecture you already know that not only beings but also substances remained behind and preserved laws which in previous planetary conditions were the right ones, and then carried those laws into the later evolution. Thus phases of evolution belonging to ancient times mingle and interpenetrate with those of modern times. And it is this which brings about such great complexities in life, which offers us the most diverse degrees of existence. The animal kingdom could never have developed alongside the human kingdom today if certain beings had not remained behind at the end of the Saturn period in order, while mankind on the Sun was already developing a stage higher, to form a second kingdom and come forward as the first ancestors of our present animal kingdom. Thus this remaining behind was absolutely necessary for subsequent developments.

A comparison may explain why beings and substances had to remain behind. The development of man had to progress by degrees, and it could only do this in the same degree to which man refined himself. Had he always worked with the same forces with which he had worked during the Saturn phase, he would not have progressed but would have remained behind. For this reason he had to refine his forces. As an illustration, let us suppose we have a glass of water in which some substance is dissolved. Everything in this glass from top to bottom will be of the same colour, the same density, etc. Now let us suppose that the grosser substances settle at the bottom; then the purer water and the finer substances remain above. The water could only be refined by separation of the grosser parts. Something like this was also necessary after the Saturn evolution had run its course, so that such a sediment appeared, and the whole of humanity separated from something, retaining all the finer parts. That which was left later formed the animal kingdom. By means of this separation man was able to refine himself, and rise a stage higher. At each step certain beings had to be separated off, in order that man could rise higher and higher.

Thus we have a humanity which has only become possible through man's freeing himself from the beings which live around him in the lower kingdoms. At one time we were bound up with these beings, with all their forces, in the flow of evolution like the denser constituents in the water. We have risen above them and in this way our development has been made possible. Thus we look down upon the three kingdoms of nature around us, and see in them something which had to become a basis for our development. These beings have sunk in order that we might be able to rise. In this manner we look upon the subordinate kingdoms of nature in the right way.

The study of the Earth development will help us to understand the details of this process still more clearly. We must be quite clear that all the facts in our earthly development have certain relationships and connections. We have seen that the separation of the Sun and Moon from the Earth really came about in order that during the Earth evolution the human organisation might be able to develop to the extent of becoming an individuality; and in conjunction with this the human organization was made pure. But through this separation in the universe for man's sake, through this great change in our solar system, the other three kingdoms of nature were also affected – especially the animal kingdom. If we wish to understand the influence exercised upon the animal kingdom through the processes of the separation of the Sun and Moon, this is what we arrive at as a result of spiritual investigation.

Man was at a certain stage of evolution when the Sun separated. Now had he been obliged to keep to this stage at which he was during the period when the Moon was still united to the Earth, he would not have been able to attain his present organization; he would have been confronted with a certain wasting and drying up. The Moon forces had first to go out. The possibility of this human organization we owe only to the circumstance that, during the period when the Moon was still part of the Earth, man had preserved an organization which could still be pliable; for it might have been possible for his organization to become so set that the exit of the Moon could no longer be of any use. Only the ancestors of humanity were at that pliable stage at which the organization was still possible. Therefore the Moon had to separate at a particular time. What took place up to the time of the exit of the Moon?

The human organization became grosser and grosser. Human beings did not, indeed, look like wood – that would be too gross a conception. The organization at that time, in spite of its grossness, was still much finer than is our present organization; but for that period between the exit of the Sun and that of the Moon, the organization of human beings was so gross that their more spiritual part, which in a certain sense lived alternately within and without the physical body, came at length to the crisis that when it wanted to re-enter its physical body it found this so dense, owing to events that had taken place on the earth, that it could no longer enter into it as its dwelling. Hence it also came about that the spiritual and soul part of many of our human ancestors departed altogether from the earth, and for a certain time took refuge on other planets belonging to our solar system. Only a small number of the physical bodies could be used and were able to maintain themselves over this time. As I have said, by far the greater number of human souls went out into space, but the onward stream of human evolution was maintained by a small number of those who were more robust and who were able to struggle and conquer. These robust souls carried the evolution over the critical period.

During the whole of this process the human individuality was still not evolved. The group soul still prevailed, and when souls withdrew they were absorbed into the being of the group soul.

Then came the exit of the Moon which made it possible for the human organization to be further refined. It could then take up the souls which had previously soared away, and these souls gradually – up to and during the Atlantean Epoch

– came down again and entered into the human bodies below. But certain organisms had reproduced themselves during this critical time and they could not become the vehicles of the human soul as they were too gross. Through this it came about that side by side with those organizations which were able to be refined and to become the vehicles of human individuality there had also been propagated organisms which could not, and these were the successors of the organisms that had been abandoned by the human soul during the time when the Sun had already withdrawn and the Moon was still united with the earth.

Thus, side by side with man, we see a kingdom of organisms actually developing, which, by preserving the Moon character, had become incapable of becoming bearers of human individualities. These organisms are essentially those which have become our present animal kingdom. It may seem curious that the grosser organisms of the present animals have certain capacities whereby they are able to act wisely, as for example in the work of the beaver. We must not conceive of these things simplistically but be quite clear about the fact that these organisms, which had not received human souls, developed the outer animal form and a nervous system, as well as other characteristics that made it possible to attain total harmony with the laws of earthly existence. For those beings which did not evolve the capacity for taking up human souls remained united with the earth the whole time. The other organisms, which later became more refined in order to take in human individualities, were also connected with the earth, but because they had to undergo certain changes later on when the Moon was outside, they lost these capacities, or rather transmuted them in refining themselves, and in having to go through other changes.

To sum up: when the Moon had split away from the Earth

certain organisms existed on Earth which carried on repro-
ducing along the lines developed when Moon and Earth were
still connected. These organisms had remained gross, had
preserved the laws which they had before, and had become so
set that when the Moon detached itself, no change took place
in them. They simply propagated without change. The other
organisms, which were to become the vehicles of human
individualities, had to change, they could not perpetuate
themselves rigidly as the grosser organisms did. They changed
in order that the spiritual beings which had not been connected with the Earth at all in the meantime, which had been
somewhere different altogether, could now work into them.
So this is the difference between the beings which had
preserved the old rigid Moon character and those which had
changed. Of what did the change consist?

When the souls which had gone away from the earth
returned and entered into physical bodies again, they began
to make alterations to the nervous system, the brain, and so
forth. They applied their forces, as it were, to inward construction. No change was possible in the other beings which
had hardened. Different beings now took hold of these latter
organisms. These beings had not yet evolved to a stage where
they could work into the inner organisms; they worked from
without like the animal group souls. Thus the organisms that
were suitably prepared received the human soul after the exit
of the Moon. And the beings pertaining to the human soul
then worked on perfecting what was to be the human organism. The organisms which had remained rigid during the
Moon period could not be changed. Beings which had not
developed far enough to attain a distinct individuality, which
had stopped evolving at the Moon stage, henceforth took
hold of these organisms as generic or group souls.

Thus we are able to grasp the difference between human

beings and animals out of the processes of the cosmos. These cosmic processes in the earth's evolution produced two kinds of organism. If we had been prevented from developing our organisms beyond the stage immediately below the human stage, our 'I' would be hovering around the earth now for want of a suitably flexible organism. We would not be able to descend, and in spite of having become more perfect beings we would have had to remain at the stage of animal group souls. But because our organisms were capable of further refinement we were able to take hold of them and make them our dwelling – in other words, we were able to descend to earth into physical bodies. The animal group souls felt no need to do this. They work into the beings concerned from out of the spiritual world.

Thus in the animal kingdom surrounding us we see something that we should also have been today, if our present organism had not been transformed. Let us now ask how the animals with their more rigid organisms have appeared on the earth. They came down through us. They are the descendants of the bodies which we no longer wished to occupy after the exit of the Moon. We left those bodies behind in order to find others later, and we should not have been able to find others later, if we had not forsaken those at that precise time. For only after the exit of the Sun could we continue our progress on the Earth. We left behind us, as it were, certain beings, in order that we ourselves might find the possibility of rising higher. In order to rise higher we had to go to other planets and leave the bodies below to go to ruin, and in a certain sense we owe what we are to what remains below. Indeed, what we 'owe' may be described in greater detail. We may ask how it was possible for us to leave the Earth during the critical period. After all, it cannot be taken for granted that beings just go where they please.

For the first time in the earth's evolution something took place that we owe to the luciferic spirits. They were our leaders and took us away from the earth evolution at the critical period. It was as though they said to us: 'Down below a critical time is now coming and you must leave the earth.' We left the earth under the guidance of the luciferic spirits, the same beings who brought into our astral body of that time the luciferic principle, the tendency in us to all that we call the possibility of evil; but with it also came the possibility of freedom. Had they not taken us away from the Earth at that time we should always have been chained to the form that we had then created, and we should now, at the most, only be able to float above that form without ever being able to enter it. So they took us away and united their own being with our being.

If we bear this in mind we shall understand that during the time we went away we took in the luciferic influences. Those other organisms which did not share in this destiny of being taken into very special regions of the world, remained down below without the luciferic influence. They had to share our earthly destiny, but they could not share our heavenly destiny. And when we came back to the earth we had the luciferic influence in us – but those other beings did not. This made it possible for us to lead a life in the physical body and yet have the possibility of becoming more and more independent of the physical body. Those other beings which did not receive the luciferic influence represent what our astral bodies were during the period between the exit of the Sun and the Moon, namely that from which we liberated ourselves. We look upon the animals and say: 'All that the animals manifest in the way of cruelty, voracity, and all animal vices, besides the skill which they have, we should have had within us, if we had not been able to eject them. We owe this liberation of our astral bodies to the circumstance that all the grosser astral bodies have remained behind in the animal kingdom of the earth.' And we can say: 'How fortunate for us that we no longer have the cruelty of the lion, the slyness of the fox within us, that these have left us to lead an independent existence outside of us.'

Thus the animals have the astral body in common with us, and are therefore able to feel pain. But from what has now been said we see that they do not possess the power to evolve through pain and through the conquest of pain, for they have no individuality. Therefore animals are far worse off than we are. We have to bear pain, but each pain is for us a means to perfection; through overcoming it we rise higher. We have left behind us the animal as something that already has the capacity to feel pain and does not yet possess the power to raise itself above pain, and to overcome it. That is the fate of the animals. They manifest to us our own former organisms when we were capable of feeling pain, but could not yet, through overcoming the pain, transform it into something beneficial for humanity. Thus in the course of our earth evolution we have left our worst aspects to the animals, and they stand around us as tokens of how we ourselves came to our perfection. We should not have got rid of the dregs if we had not left the animals behind.

We must learn to consider such facts, not as theories, but rather with a cosmic world feeling. When we look upon the animals we should feel: 'You animals are outside. When you suffer, you suffer something of which we reap the benefit. We human beings, however, have the power to overcome suffering while you must endure it. We have left the suffering to you, and have taken the power to overcome it.'

If we develop this cosmic feeling out of the theory it will grow into an all-encompassing sense of compassion for the animal kingdom. Hence when this universal feeling sprang from the primeval wisdom of humanity, when mankind still possessed the remembrance of the primeval wisdom which told each one by a dim clairvoyant vision how things once were, the sense of compassion for the animal kingdom was equally preserved, and this sense of compassion was very highly developed indeed. It will come again when people accustom themselves to take up spiritual science, and when they understand once more how the karma of humanity is bound up with the world karma. In the so-called Dark Ages when materialistic thought held sway these connections could not be understood. At that time one observed only what was side by side in space, without taking into consideration the fact that whatever is side by side in space has a common origin, and has only separated in the course of evolution. And naturally there was no feeling either of any connection between the human being and the animal. And in those parts of the earth where the mission was to cover up the consciousness of man's connection with the animal world, where it was replaced by a consciousness limited to external physical space, human beings have been paying their debt to the animals in a strange fashion – by eating them.

However, these things also show us how the various views of the world are related to the world of human sensation and feeling. After all, sensations and feelings are a consequence of prevailing views of the world, and as concepts and ideas change, humanity's sensations and feelings change. The human being could not do otherwise but evolve; other beings had to be pushed into the abyss to make possible the ascent of the human being. The human being could not give the animals an individuality which compensates karmically for what the animals have to suffer; he could only give them the pain, without the karmic law of compensation. However, when the human being has attained the freedom and selflessness of his individuality, he will be able to give them what he could not give them in earlier times. Then he will – in a conscious way – grasp the karmic law in this realm, too, and he will say: 'It is to the animals that I owe what I have now become. What I cannot give any more to individual animal beings which have descended from an individual existence to a shadow existence, what I have once incurred in debt to the animal, as it were, I have to make good now towards the animals through the very way I treat them!' Therefore, with the progress of evolution, through the knowledge of karma, the human being's relationship to the animal world will progress, too, beyond what it is now, especially in the West. The human being will raise up again what he cast down, and this will be reflected in his treatment of the animals.

Thus we see that there is a certain relationship between karma and the animal kingdom, although we must not confuse matters by likening what the animal experiences as its fate with human karma. But if we consider the whole earth development, and what had to come about for the sake of humanity and its evolution, we will see that we can indeed speak of a relationship between the karma of humanity and the animal kingdom.

LECTURE 3

Karma in Relation to Health and Illness

Hamburg, 18 May 1910

What we shall deal with now and in the next few days could give rise to misunderstandings. I will speak about certain questions of illness and health from the point of view of karma, and as present-day views on this subject diverge so widely, there is a certain risk that the fundamental ideas of spiritual science will be misunderstood when the relationship of illness and health with karma is discussed. You are surely aware of the intensity and passion with which questions of health and illness are discussed in the widest circles. You will all be familiar with the opposition voiced by non-experts as well as certain members of the medical profession against what is called scientific medicine. On the other hand it is obvious that the representatives of scientific medicine frequently feel challenged by many an unjustified attack to do more than defend the scientific point of view with passion. Some of them have embarked on a real battle against whatever may be put forward on the subject of health and illness from any angle different from that of official medicine. Anthroposophy or spiritual science will only do justice to its great tasks if it succeeds in maintaining an unprejudiced and objective judgement in questions like this, where a great deal of confusion is created by endless discussions. Anyone who has attended similar lectures of mine will know how little I am inclined to join in the chorus of those who wish to discredit what is called 'conventional medicine'. Spiritual science is very far from wishing to join any particular body of opinion.

Allow me to take this opportunity to stress right from the beginning that the factual accomplishments and research efforts of recent years and decades, particularly in the field of human illness and health, are worthy of praise, recognition and admiration – as are numerous other endeavours of natural science. And concerning what has actually been achieved in this field I may also say that if anyone has reason to rejoice over what has been achieved by medicine in recent years, it is spiritual science. However, it must be equally emphasised – and this applies to natural science in particular – that the achievements, the actual knowledge gained and the discoveries which are made are rarely interpreted and explained satisfactorily by present-day scientific opinion. This is a striking feature of many spheres of scientific research today: the opinions and theories which are put forward do not match up to the objective facts, some of which are miraculous. Only the light of spiritual science will bring a clear understanding of what has been achieved in this field in recent years.

It should be quite clear now that we are not in the slightest concerned with joining any paltry opposition to present endeavours in scientific medicine. At the same time it must be pointed out that the admirable facts which have come to light will not be able to bear fruit for the good of mankind in our time because they are rendered fruitless by today's materialistic opinions and theories. For this reason, it is far more appropriate for anthroposophy unpretentiously to say what needs to be said than to engage in any sort of 'party squabble'. Such an approach will at least not ignite matters any further.

To reach any point of view at all from which to consider the questions before us we need to be clear about the fact that the causes of any phenomenon must be researched in a great variety of ways; some are close, others very remote, and when the karmic causes of health-related matters are researched by means of anthroposophy, it is the more remote causes, those which are not right on the surface, which we need to look at primarily. I will give you a comparison which will make things clearer. If you think it through you will certainly discover what I mean.

Let us assume that someone took the view, 'How splendidly we have advanced in this field today,' while patently ignoring all the previous centuries' research on health and illness. If you attempted to form some kind of general view of what is said about health and illness today, you would find something like this view prevailing among the experts: What has emerged in this field in the last twenty or thirty years is a kind of absolute truth which may be expanded but could most certainly never be refuted or judged negatively, as is most of what human endeavour had previously brought to light in the discipline concerned – such judgements unfortunately often being pronounced by the proclaimers of the new truth! So it is said for example: 'Especially in this field there was gross superstition in the olden days' – and this is followed by frightening examples of how people attempted to heal this or that complaint in previous centuries. Such judgements become even more extreme when expressions are found in some context or other whose original meaning is no longer available to modern-day consciousness but which have nevertheless crept into it. For example someone might say: 'There were times when every illness was attributed to God or the devil!' Things were not as bad as such people make out because they have no idea of the complex ideas encapsulated in expressions such as 'God' or 'devil'. The following example will illustrate this.

Let us assume that two people are talking to each other. One says to the other: 'I have just seen a room full of flies. Someone said it was quite natural the room should be full of flies, and I thought so too, for the room was very dirty, and so the flies thrive.'

'It really makes sense to consider this the reason for the existence of flies and I, too, believe that the one who says that the flies will not be in the room once it is cleaned thoroughly is right!' But now another person comes along and says that he knows another reason why so many flies were in the room; and that the real cause was that a bone-idle housewife had lived there for a long time. Now, what boundless superstition to think that idleness is like a kind of person who only needs to beckon and in come the flies! Surely the other explanation which attributes the presence of flies to the dirt is more correct!

The case is similar in an altogether different context when it is said: 'Someone has fallen ill as a result of being infected by some sort of bacillus; if this is driven out he will be well again.' But now there are others who speak of some kind of spiritual cause which lies deeper down! Surely all one needs to do is drive out the bacillus. To speak of a spiritual cause of illness while admitting all the rest is no more superstitious than considering a bone-idle housewife to be the cause of the presence of flies. And there is no need to be angry if someone says that the flies would not be there if the room were clean. It is not a question of one view being in opposition to the other; it is more important to try and understand each other's point of view and intention. One must carefully take into consideration whether only the immediate causes are spoken of, or whether indirect causes are referred to. The objective anthroposophist will never take the standpoint that laziness needs only to beckon for the flies to come into the room; he will know that other material things also come into consideration. Everything which has a material expression has its spiritual background, and for the welfare of humanity this spiritual background has to be sought. Those, however, who would rather join the battle of arguments should also be reminded that spiritual causes are highly differentiated and also cannot be combated in the same way as ordinary material causes; it would also be wrong to think that fighting the spiritual causes obviates the need to fight the material causes, for then one might allow the room to remain dirty and only seek to cure the idleness of the housewife.

Looking at karma we have to consider the connection between events that happened earlier in a person's life and their effect on the same person at a later time. In relation to health and illness from the point of view of karma that means nothing but this: Can we connect the healthy and diseased condition with the former deeds and experiences of this person, and how will his present condition of health or disease later react upon him?

Nowadays people would far rather believe that illness is connected only with immediate causes. For the fundamental tendency in the modern view of life is to seek always what is most convenient. And it is certainly convenient to go no further than the immediate cause. Therefore especially in relation to illness only the immediate causes are taken into consideration – and this applies most of all to those afflicted with the illness. For it cannot be denied that the patients themselves are led to take this standpoint, and because of this there exists so much dissatisfaction when there is a belief that the disease must have an immediate cause which must be found by the skilled physician. If he cannot help, he is accused of having bungled somehow. From this convenient method of judgement proceeds much of what is said at the present time on this subject. If our understanding of the concept of karma really comprises its wide-ranging effects we will gradually expand our view from the events of the present moment to those that happened a lot earlier, in relative terms. What is more important, we will know for sure that matters relating to human life cannot be properly understood unless we expand our view to encompass what happened further back in time. This applies particularly to the question of illness.

When we talk about someone who is ill, or healthy for that matter, the pressing question will always be: How can we form any idea of this state of ill-health?

Spiritual-scientific research, when applied directly and with the help of clairvoyant faculties to a phenomenon of human illness, will always note certain irregularities; these will not only be found in the physical body of the person concerned but also in his higher members, in his etheric and astral bodies. Due to the fact that all three members can be implicated in the illness, the clairvoyant researcher will always have to consider what part the physical body on the one hand, and the etheric and astral bodies on the other, play in the case concerned. This raises the question as to the ideas we might form about the origins of the illness. For that purpose we need to define the actual concept of illness. There are people who like to speak of all sorts of matters in allegorical-symbolical terms and accordingly refer to the illnesses of even minerals or metals; hence rust eating away at iron would be defined as a process of illness. People may think as they wish but we must be quite clear about the fact that life cannot really be grasped fruitfully with such abstract thinking; one might arrive at some kind of playful notion of life which has nothing to do with actual facts. If we want to arrive at a proper concept of illness and indeed health we must refrain from speaking of minerals and metals in terms of falling ill.

In the plant world, however, matters are quite different. It is certainly possible to speak of plants having illnesses. Indeed, diseases of plants are of great interest and of supreme relevance when it comes to grasping the concept of illness. Leaving any playful conceptualization aside one cannot really speak of inner causes of illness in the case of plants, as one may very well do in the case of the animal or the human being. Diseases of plants must always be traced to outer causes, to this or that detrimental effect of the earth, insufficient light, effects of the wind and other forces of the elements and nature. Diseases of plants may furthermore be traced to the influence of parasites that attack the plants and damage them. To speak of 'inner causes of illness' in relation to plants is basically totally unjustified. As I do not have half a year available to speak about this subject it is impossible for me to furnish innumerable proofs of what I have just indicated. However, the more deeply we penetrate into plant pathology the more clearly we will understand that the concept of 'inner causes of illness' is simply not applicable to plants and that their diseases are caused by outer phenomena and damaging outer influences.

A plant is a being which consists of a physical body and an etheric body, and this is how we first encounter it in the outer world. At the same time this being draws our attention to the fact, as it were, that such a being which consists of physical and etheric body is healthy in principle and will only fall ill in response to an outer injury. This fully accords with the findings of spiritual science. In the case of animal or human illness definite changes in the inner or supersensible regions of the organism may be discovered by clairvoyant research, but this will never be found in plants; in a diseased plant it is not the original etheric body which is changed, but certain disturbances and harmful influences have forced their way into the physical body and especially the etheric body from outside. The results of spiritual research fully validate the general conclusion that the plant, consisting of physical body and etheric body, is in essence healthy. A further important aspect is the plant's capacity, on receiving outside injuries, to mobilize all kinds of defences to safeguard its growth and development, to heal itself. Notice for instance how, if you cut a plant, it tries to grow around the damaged part, to by-pass whatever may be obstructing and damaging it. We can almost see the plant's inner defence system, its healing power, become activated.

So there is something in the plant's etheric and physical body which is capable of activating inner healing forces in response to outer injury. This is an extremely important fact to consider. A being such as a plant, consisting of etheric and physical body, not only shows us that the physical body and the etheric body have sufficient inherent health to ensure the development and growth of the being concerned, but that there is even a superabundance of such forces which can be activated for healing when external damage occurs. Where do these healing forces originate?

If you wound a merely physical body the injury will remain; it is unable of itself to repair the injury. For this reason, we cannot talk of a disease in the case of a merely physical body, and least of all can we talk of a relation between disease and healing. This we can best see when a disease appears in a plant. Here we have to look for the principle of the inner healing power in the etheric body. Spiritual investigation shows us this very clearly, for the activity of the etheric body of the plant is much intensified around the part where the wound has been inflicted. The etheric body produces completely different forms then, it flows in a very different way. It is an extremely interesting fact that we challenge the etheric body of a plant to increased activity when we injure its physical body.

Whilst this is not a definition of the concept of illness, it does give us an idea of the processes involved in illness as well as of the inner nature of healing.

Following the clue given by inward spiritual observation let us go further and try to understand the external phenomena to which spiritual science leads us. Let us now consider injuries inflicted on animals – beings that have an astral body. If we carry our observations further we shall see that the etheric body of a higher animal reacts correspondingly less to an external injury. The higher the animal is in the scale of evolution so much the less will be the activity of the etheric body. If we cause a severe injury to the physical body of a lower or even a higher mammal, if, for instance, we tear a leg off a dog or some such animal, we find that the etheric body cannot respond with its healing power in the same measure as the etheric body of a plant responds to a similar injury to itself. But even in the animal kingdom this activity of the etheric body can still be seen to a great extent. Let us descend to a very low order of animals, to the tritons. If we cut off certain organs from such a creature it will not experience anything particularly painful. The organs quickly grow again, and the animal soon looks as it did before. In this case something similar has taken place as in the case of the plant; we have called forth a certain healing power in the etheric body. But it cannot be denied that such provocation to develop healing powers in the etheric body of the human being or of higher animals would constitute a considerable risk to health. The lower animal on the contrary will only be stimulated from its inner being to put forth another member by means of its etheric body.

If one of the limbs of a crab is severed, the animal cannot at once renew it. But when it casts its shell the next time and arrives at the next transition stage of its life, a stump appears; the second time the stump grows larger, and if the animal were to cast its shell often enough, the limb would be replaced by a new one. These facts show us that the etheric body must make greater efforts to call forth the inner forces of healing; and in the higher animals the healing power is still less. If you mutilate a higher animal it cannot initially bring forth this healing power from out of its etheric body. Yet, the following is true, and I would like to emphasize this point which is the subject of a major dispute in scientific circles today: if you mutilate an animal, and the animal has progeny, the deformities are not transmitted to the offspring; the next generation has again the complete parts. When the etheric body carries its qualities over to the offspring it is again stimulated to form a complete organism. The etheric body of a triton still acts in the same animal; in a crab it acts only when it casts its shell; in the higher animals the same phenomenon appears only in the offspring, and there the etheric body replaces what had been mutilated in the previous generation. Therefore it is essential that we observe such phenomena in nature carefully and step by step; then it will become clear that the principle of the etheric body's healing forces always applies, even if they only manifest in the succeeding generation when the offspring of a mutilated animal is born intact and whole. Here we have, as it were, research into the whys and wherefores of the healing powers of the etheric body.

We might now ask the question: how is it, then, that the higher we rise in the animal kingdom – and this applies externally to the human kingdom also – we find that the healing forces of the etheric body have to make greater efforts to manifest themselves? This has to do with the many different ways in which the etheric body can be connected with the physical body. Between the physical body and the etheric body there may be a more intimate union or a loose one. For example, let us take the triton, in which the severed member is replaced very quickly. Here we must assume a loose connection between the physical body and the etheric body, and this applies in the plant kingdom to a still higher degree. This union, let us say, is such that the physical body is unable to react upon the etheric body, and the latter remains untouched by what happens to the physical body and is in a certain sense independent of it. Now the nature of the etheric body is that of activity, of generation and growth. It encourages growth up to a certain point. When we cut off a part of a plant or of one of the lower animals, the etheric body is immediately prepared to restore that part, and to that end unfolds all its activities. But what is the reason if it cannot develop all its activities? The reason is to be found in a closer dependence on the physical body. This is the case with the higher animals. There is a much more intimate connection between the etheric body and the physical body, and when the physical body develops its form and organizes the forces of physical nature, these forces react upon the etheric body.

To put it clearly: in the lower animals or the plants, that which is outside does not react on the etheric body but leaves it untouched, carrying on an independent existence. When we come to the higher animals, reactions of the physical body are imposed upon the etheric body which adapts itself completely to the physical body; so that if we injure the physical body, we injure the etheric body at the same time. Hence the etheric body has to exercise greater powers as it has to first heal itself and then the corresponding member in the physical body. Therefore in the case of the etheric body of a higher animal, deeper healing forces must be called forth. But what is the connection? Why is the etheric body of a higher animal so dependent upon the forms of the physical body?

The higher we advance in animal creation the more we need to take into account the activity of the astral body besides that of the etheric and physical body. In the case of the lower animals the activity of the astral body is extremely limited. For this reason the lower animals still have so many qualities in common with the plants. The higher we ascend, the more does the astral body come into action, and this action is such that it makes the etheric body subservient to itself. A being such as a plant, which has only physical body and etheric body, has little to do with the external world; certain stimuli may be exercised upon the plant from outside, but they are not reflected as inner processes. Where an astral body is active, external impressions are reflected in inner experiences, but a being in which the astral body is inactive is more shut off from the external world. The greater the activity of the astral body the greater is that creature's openness to the outer world. Thus the astral body unites the inner nature of a being with the outer world, and the increasing activity of the astral body brings it about that the etheric body has to use much stronger forces to make injuries good.

If we now pass on from the animal to the human being a new element arises. Man does not simply conform to certain prescribed functions inspired by the astral body as is the case with the animals which have, as it were, a course outlined for them in advance, and which live more according to an established programme. We could scarcely say of an animal that it is given to excess in relation to its instincts, or that it follows its instincts with more or less moderation. It follows its plan of life, and all its actions are subject to a sort of typical programme. But the human being, having risen higher on the ladder of evolution, is able to discern between right and wrong, truth and falsehood, good and evil. He comes into contact with the world outside in countless different ways and for many purely individual reasons. All these kinds of contact react and make an impression upon his astral body, and as a consequence of the interaction between his astral body and etheric body, both now suffer these reactions. Thus if a person leads a dissolute life in any respect it will make an impression on his astral body which in its turn influences the etheric body. How it will do this will depend upon what has been laid down in the astral body. This will enable us to understand that our etheric body changes in accordance with the kind of life we lead within the boundaries of good and evil, right or wrong, truth or untruth, and so forth.

Let us now remember what takes place when a human being passes through the portal of death. We know that the physical body is laid aside and that the etheric body, now united with the astral body and the 'I', remains. When a certain length of time has elapsed after death, a time which is measured only by days, the etheric body is thrown aside as a second corpse; an extract, however, of the etheric body is left over and this is taken along and kept permanently. In this extract of the etheric body is contained, as if in an essence, all that has penetrated the etheric body, for example, from a dissolute life, or from true or false thinking, feeling and action. This is contained in the etheric body and the human being concerned takes it with him into the period up to a new birth. As an animal does not have such experiences, it cannot, of course, take anything over in the same way beyond the portal of death. When a human being comes into existence again through birth, the essence of his previous etheric body now impregnates his new etheric body and permeates its structure. Therefore in his new existence the person has in his etheric body the results of what he had experienced in his previous life, and as the etheric body is the builder of an entirely new organization at a new birth, all this now imprints itself on his physical body also. How does this come about?

Spiritual investigation shows us that in the form of a human body which enters into existence through birth we are able to see approximately what a person did in a previous life. But will we also find a really reasonable explanation for what we established as diminishing healing power in the ascending forms of animal species? In the case of an animal we cannot say that at its birth it brings with it a reincarnated individuality from a previous earth life. Only the common astral body of this species of animal is active, and this will limit the healing power of the etheric body of this animal. In contrast we find that in the case of the human being not only his astral body but also his etheric body is impregnated with the results of the deeds of his previous life: and as the etheric body has within itself the power to bring forth what it formerly had, we shall also understand that this etheric body will also build into the new organism that which it brings with it from previous incarnations. Now we understand how our deeds in one life can work over into our state of health in the next life, and how in our state of health we have often to seek a karmic effect of our previous life's deeds.

We may approach the matter in yet another way. We may ask: 'Does everything that we do in the life between birth and death react in the same manner on our etheric body?' Even in ordinary life we can perceive a great difference in our inner organization between the reaction of what we experience as conscious beings, and many other experiences. Here we are dealing with an extremely interesting fact which can be fully explained by spiritual science but can also be understood with ordinary powers of reason. In the course of his life a person has a great number of experiences which he receives consciously and unites with his 'I'. Within him they develop into mental representations which he works upon, etc. But just think of the infinite number of experiences and impressions which never actually develop into mental representations and are nevertheless part of us and affect us.[1] It will often happen that someone says to you: 'I saw you in the street today; you even looked at me!' – and you know nothing about it; it is a common experience. Of course, this has made an impression; your eyes indeed saw the other person but the immediate impression did not develop into a mental image. There are countless impressions of this sort, so that our life is really divided into two parts – into a realm of soul-life which consists of conscious mental images and another realm that we have never brought really into clear consciousness. But there are further differences. You will easily be able to distinguish between impressions which you have had in your life and can remember, and those which you cannot remember.

Thus our soul-life is divided into entirely different categories, and there is, indeed, a very considerable difference between these various categories if we consider the effect upon the inner being of man. Let us now dwell for a while on the life of the human being between birth and death. First of all we observe this great difference between the mental images which can emerge in our consciousness again and again, and those which have been forgotten and in relation to which the ability of being recalled has not actually developed. This difference can be most easily exemplified by the following. Think of an impression which called forth a clear idea or mental image within you. Let it be an impression which aroused joy or pain, an impression which was accompanied by a feeling. Let us bear in mind that most impressions

– really all the impressions that are made upon us – are accompanied by feelings and these feelings express themselves not only on the conscious surface of life but work deeply into the physical body. You need only remember how one impression will cause us to become pale, and another causes us to blush. These impressions affect the circulation of the blood. And now let us pass over to what on the whole does not come to consciousness, or only fleetingly so, and is not remembered. Spiritual science shows us that such impressions are none the less accompanied by emotions in the same way as the conscious ones. If you receive an impression from the outer world which, if received consciously, would have frightened you so much that it would have made your heart pound, that same impression will still affect you even if it is received unconsciously. It not only makes an impression, but it also works into the physical body. It is remarkable that an impression which produces a conscious idea or mental image finds a kind of resistance when working into the deeper human organization; but if the impression simply acts upon us without our bringing it to a conscious idea, then nothing hinders it, but that renders it no less effective. Our human life is very much richer than what actually reaches our consciousness. In the entire period from birth until the time when memory begins we receive an infinite number of rich impressions which all stay within us and which change us in the course of that period. They work into the human being in the same way as the conscious impressions but there is nothing opposed to them, especially when they are forgotten. Nothing that is otherwise contained in the soul-life in the way of conscious mental images can thereby form a dam, as it were, and the subconscious impressions are those which act most profoundly. Life itself provides us with many examples which fully confirm that there are moments in the life of a human being when the second type of inner effect is manifested. We all experience things in our lives which we find hard to understand. There are many situations which leave you wondering why on earth you had to go through them when you did. For example, some impression or other might move you in a way that seems utterly incomprehensible, and makes you wonder why such a relatively insignificant experience could shock you that much. If you looked into the matter you might find that during that critical period – between birth and the time to which our memory extends back – you had a similar experience which was, however, forgotten. You have not retained any picture of it which you could call to mind. The impression at the time was shocking; this lives on and now merges with the present impression, which it reinforces. And what would otherwise have moved or shocked you a lot less now leaves a particularly potent impression. Once this becomes clear to you, you will grasp the infinitely great responsibility involved in bringing up a child in its earliest years; you will understand how everything will cast its shadow or light into the subsequent life of the individual concerned in a most significant manner. In this way something of an earlier stage of life works into the later stages of that life.

Now it may turn out that such impressions received in childhood – especially if they recurred frequently – affect the individual's entire disposition towards life; for example, a person might succumb to a depressed mood which is inexplicable, and can only be explained by looking back to find out what kind of impressions from an earlier period are throwing their lights or shadows into the individual's later life, for it is these which now manifest as depression. It will furthermore turn out that events which did not just pass the child by, but left a strong impression on him even then, will have a particularly strong effect. In other words: when impressions that are later forgotten strongly involved the feeling life, these strong emotions and intense feelings will be especially effective in calling forth similar experiences later on.

You may remember what I have said on various occasions about life during the time of kamaloca. After the etheric body has been cast aside as a second corpse, the human being lives through his entire life in reverse order, reliving everything he experienced in that last life. What he thus experiences leaves him by no means indifferent. Especially during the period of kamaloca that which is lived through engenders very profound feelings, as the human being still possesses his old astral body. Let us assume for instance that somebody died at the age of seventy and lives his life backwards to his fortieth year, when he struck someone in the face. He then experiences the pain he caused the other. This produces a kind of self-reproach; from this the person retains a longing which he takes with him into his next life – a longing to make good this deed in his next life. You will understand that due to such astral experiences between death and a new birth our experiences of outer actions are imprinted all the more deeply and unfailingly into our inner being and affect the constitution of our new body. In other words, if in ordinary life we can be touched so strongly by certain experiences – especially in the case of impressions on our feeling life – that our state of mind is adversely affected, we will understand that the very much more intense impressions received during kamaloca can work right down into the structure of the physical body in a new incarnation.

This is an accentuated form of a phenomenon which you may already observe in life between birth and death, provided that you look carefully. Impressions which meet with no hindrance through consciousness will tend to lead to irregularities in the soul: neurasthenia, various kinds of nervous disorders, even mental illness at times. All these phenomena clearly point us to causal connections between earlier and later events.

Developing this concept further we can say that our deeds in one life will be transformed into a powerful emotion after death. This emotion – which is not diluted now by any mental image involving the physical body, by no ordinary consciousness, as the brain is not necessary for this – and which is now experienced through the other, deeper form of consciousness, brings it about that our deeds and the total quality of our being in our previous life, are now reflected in our disposition and physical structure in a new life. We will understand that a person inclined to self-centredness in his thinking, feeling and willing during his last incarnation will be suffused with powerful emotions against his earlier deeds when confronted with the fruits of his egotistical thinking, feeling and willing after death. This is indeed the case. He will develop certain inner tendencies which are directed against his own being. And in so far as such tendencies have been produced by the quality of egotism in his previous life they will be expressed in a weak organization in the next. By 'weak organization' I am referring to the inner nature, not the outward impression. We need to be clear about the fact that a weak organization can be traced back karmically to egotism in a previous life.

Let us go further. Let us suppose that in one life a person manifests a particular tendency towards telling lies. This is indeed a tendency which originates in deeper layers of the soul; for if a person is guided only by what is in his clearest consciousness he will not really lie. It is only emotions and feelings which work up out of his subconscious which lead him to this. It is a question of something more deep-seated.

If a person is untruthful, the actions which proceed from untruthfulness will again arouse the most forcible feelings against himself in the life after death, and a marked inclination against lying will emerge. He will then bring with him into his next life not only a weak organization but – so spiritual science shows – an organization which is incorrectly built, so to speak, and which manifests irregularly formed inner organs in the finer organization. Something is not quite balanced and this is due to the earlier tendency to lying. And where did this tendency to lying itself come from? After all, in that tendency the person already possesses something which is irregular.

We need to go back further still to answer this question. Spiritual science shows that a life which knows neither devotion nor love – a superficial life in one incarnation – expresses itself in the tendency to lying in the next incarnation; and in the third incarnation this tendency to lying manifests itself in incorrectly formed organs. Thus we can karmically trace the effects in three consecutive incarnations: superficiality and unsteadiness in the first incarnation, the tendency to lying in the second, and the physical disposition to illness in the third incarnation. This shows us how karma is connected with health and illness.

At the beginning of this lecture we dealt with the most obvious facts: the healing forces of plants' etheric bodies. We then showed how the astral body which the animal possesses in addition to the etheric renders the latter less effective; we further learnt that the astral body which in the ascending order of animal species only inhibits the healing forces, affords something new to the human being through carrying the 'I' which enables the development of an individual life within the boundaries of good and evil, truth and falsity: the karmic effects on health and illness that originate in man's individual life. In the case of the plant there are no inner causes of illness because illness is still something outside and the etheric healing forces work unhindered. In the lower animals the etheric body's healing forces still work to the extent where certain parts can be restored; but the higher we ascend the more strongly the astral body imprints itself into the etheric body, thereby limiting the etheric body's healing forces. Yet, as the animal does not propagate through reincarnation, the content of the animal's etheric body is not associated with any moral-intellectual or individual qualities but rather with the general type of the species. However, in the case of the human being that which he experiences in his 'I' in the period between birth and death works right down into the etheric body.

Why do the experiences of childhood in relation to the effects on the feeling life described only manifest as lighter forms of illness? Because much of what emerges in the form of neurasthenia, neurosis, hysteria and so forth is caused by things that happened during the same life. However, the causes of more severe forms of illness must be sought in one or the other previous incarnation, because whatever is experienced morally and intellectually can only be fully implanted in the etheric body on passing over to a new birth. On the whole, the human etheric body cannot embody the deeper moral activities in one life, although we shall still hear of exceptional cases, and indeed of very important ones.

Such is the connection which exists between our life of good or evil, our moral and intellectual life in one incarnation, and our state of health or illness in the next.

LECTURE 4

Karma in Relation to the Curability and Incurability of Diseases

Hamburg, 19 May 1910

With regard to the two themes of today's lecture – the curability and incurability of illnesses – clearer ideas and concepts more acceptable to humanity will prevail when the concepts of karma and karmic connections in life will have been accepted by wider circles. It is a fact that there have been widely divergent views on the question of the curability and incurability of illnesses in the various centuries. And we don't need to go back very far to see how tremendously these concepts have changed.

We find a time at the turning point between the Middle Ages and modern times, about the sixteenth to the seventeenth century, when the idea gradually gained ground that the various forms of illness could be strictly delimited, and that for every disease there was some sort of herb or mixture by which it could be cured without fail. This belief lasted for a long time, even into the nineteenth century. When we as laymen, or as people who have absorbed present day ideas on the subject, read accounts of medical treatments from the end of the eighteenth or the beginning of the nineteenth centuries, and for some time later, we are astounded at all the remedies and recipes in general use at that time: teas, mixtures, more dangerous medicines, blood-letting, and so on.

Yet it was also in the nineteenth century that this approach was reversed into its exact opposite in medical circles, and indeed in distinguished medical circles. I may add that I came across a great variety of these opposing views in my younger years. There was plenty of opportunity to witness such phenomena in the context of the 'nihilistic school of medicine' which was started in Vienna around the middle of the nineteenth century and won more and more favour. A radical change in the views on curability and incurability set in when the renowned physician Dietl brought to light his findings on the process of pneumonia and similar diseases.[1] From all kinds of observations he arrived at the conclusion that fundamentally there was no real effect to be noticed from the use of various remedies on the course of one disease or another. Under the influence of Dietl's school, the young doctors of that day acquired a way of thinking in relation to the healing value of the remedies which had been used for centuries that almost outdid what is conveyed in the well-known saying: When the cock crows on the dung-heap the weather will change – or it will remain as it is! They were of the opinion that it made little difference to the course of any disease whether one administered a certain remedy or not. Dietl managed to produce some statistics – which were quite convincing at the time – and showed that in his so-called 'wait-and-see' treatment, roughly the same number of people suffering from pneumonia were cured or died as in earlier forms of treatment with time-honoured remedies. The temporizing therapy established by Dietl, and continued by Skoda,[2] was based on bringing the patient into a condition in which he was best able to stimulate the self-healing powers and to draw them forth from his organism. The doctor had little more to do than watch the course of the disease and to be at hand if anything happened, so that he could give assistance in a practical way. For the rest he confined himself to watching the disease come, as it were, and waiting to see how the self-healing forces came out of the organism, until after a time the fever subsided and self-healing came about.

This school of medicine was called, and is still called, 'The Nihilistic School', because it rested on a statement by Professor Skoda who said something like: We may perhaps learn to diagnose diseases, to describe them, perhaps even explain them – but we cannot heal them! I am telling you these things so that you may take note of them as actual developments in the course of the nineteenth century; my aim is to give you an idea of how views in this field have changed. But because these things are related in purely narrative form it is not implied that you should take sides in any way; for obviously the statement of the celebrated Professor Skoda was a kind of radicalism and it would be easy to define the limits of its validity. There was, however, one point or aspect which was repeatedly emphasized by this particular school of medicine. Although they had no means of proving it and had not even the words to describe exactly the content of their conception, they repeatedly affirmed that there must be in the human being some element which determines the appearance and the course of his illness, and which is fundamentally beyond the reach of any help others can give.

Thus a reference was made to something beyond human aid; and if one really gets to the bottom of these things, this indication cannot relate to anything other than the law of karma and its activity in human life. If we follow the course of an illness in human life, how it develops, and how the healing powers spring forth from the organism itself; if we follow the process of healing impartially – particularly if we consider how in one case a cure takes place, while in another it fails – we shall be driven to search for a deeper law determining this. Can this deeper law be sought for in the previous earth-life of man? That is our question. Can we say that a person brings with him certain predispositions which in one particular case called forth the healing powers from his organism, but which in another case, in spite of every effort, held these forces back?

If you remember what I told you yesterday, you will understand that very special forces indeed are taken into the human individuality in the time between death and a new birth. During the period in kamaloca the events of a person's last life, his good and bad deeds, his moral qualities, and so on, come before his soul, and through contemplating his own life in this way he acquires the inclination to bring about the remedy and compensation for all that is imperfect in him, and which has manifested as wrong action. He is moved to acquire those qualities which will bring him nearer to perfection in various directions. He forms intentions and tendencies during the time up to a new birth, and goes into existence again with these intentions. Further, he himself works upon the new body which he acquires for his new life, and he builds it in conformity with the forces he has brought from previous earthly lives, and from the time between death and rebirth. He is furnished with these forces, and builds them into his new body. From this it may be seen that this new body will be weak or strong in accordance with the individual's capacity to build weak or strong forces into it.

Now it must be clearly understood that a certain sequence of events sets in when, for example, during the life in kamaloca, a person sees that in his last life, he frequently acted under the influence of the emotions of anger, fear, aversion, and so on. These actions now stand vividly before his soul in kamaloca, and in his soul is formed the thought (the expressions which we have to use for these forces are of course coined from the physical life): 'I must do something to myself, so that I will become more perfect in this respect, so that in the future I will no longer be inclined to commit such actions under the dominance of my emotions.' This thought becomes an integral part of the human soul individuality, and during the passage through to a new birth it is imprinted still further as a force in the new body. Thus this new body is penetrated with the tendency so to act on the whole organization of the physical body, the etheric body and astral body, that it will be prevented from performing certain actions resulting from the emotions of anger, hate, envy, and so on. The person will be impelled to fresh actions which will compensate for previous ones. Thus from a reason which extends far beyond his ordinary rationality, the person is imbued with a strong desire for a higher perfection in certain directions, and with the desire also to compensate for certain deeds. If we consider how manifold life is, and how day by day we perform actions which require compensation of this sort, we shall understand that, when the soul enters into existence through a new birth, it contains many such thoughts waiting to be balanced, and that these manifold thoughts and tendencies cross one another, making the human physical body and etheric body receive a complex warp and woof of such tendencies and desires. To illustrate this, let us take a striking case, and I must again repeat that I avoid speaking from any sort of theory or hypothesis, and that when I give examples I give only those that have been tested by spiritual science.

Let us suppose that in his previous life a person acted from an 'I'-feeling which was much too weak, and which permitted far too great an openness to the outer world, so great that it gave to his actions a lack of independence, a lack of character which no longer fits the present state of humanity. Thus it was this lack of feeling of self which led him in one incarnation to perform certain actions. During the kamaloca period he had before him the actions which proceeded from this atrophy of his 'I' and from this he acquires the tendency: 'I must develop within me forces which strengthen my sense of self; in my next incarnation I must seek for opportunities to strengthen this sense, to train it, as it were, against the opposition of my body, against the forces which will come to me in my next incarnation from my physical body, etheric body and astral body. I must make a body which will show me the consequences of a weak personality!'

The effect of this in the next incarnation will not fully enter into consciousness; it will run its course more or less in a subconscious region. The person in question will strive for an incarnation in which he will encounter the greatest opposition to his 'I'-consciousness, so that he has to exert these feelings to the highest degree. This striving draws him, as if magnetically, to places and circumstances where he meets with great hindrances, so that his 'I' is stimulated into action in opposition to the organization of the three bodies. Strange as it may sound, the individualities who have this karma, coming into existence by birth in the way we have described, seek opportunities where, for instance, they will be exposed to an epidemic such as cholera, for this gives them the opportunity of meeting with the opposition we have described above. The activity which is thus experienced in the inner being of the person who is ill owing to the opposition of the three bodies can then so work that in the next incarnation his feeling of self will be much stronger.

Let us take another extreme case, and to make the connection quite clear we will assume the exact opposite. During the kamaloca period a person sees that he has acted from too strong a feeling of self. He sees that he must be more temperate as regards this feeling and that he must subdue it. So he will seek an opportunity whereby in the next incarnation his threefold organism will so condition him that his 'I'-consciousness, however much it strives, will find no limitations, and he will be led to the unfathomable and to absurdity. These opportunities come to him when karma brings him malaria.

Here you have a case of disease brought about by karma which explains that fundamentally man is led by a higher kind of reason than he perceives with his ordinary consciousness to circumstances which in the course of his karma are favourable to his development. If we bear in mind what has just been said, we shall find it much easier to understand the epidemic nature of diseases. We could bring forward many different examples showing how, because of his experience in the kamaloca period, a human being actually seeks for the opportunity to get a certain illness, in order that by overcoming it and by developing the self-healing forces he may gain strength and power which will lead him upward on the path of evolution.

I said previously that if a person has done many things under the influence of his passions he will in the kamaloca period live through actions which have also come about under such an influence. This will arouse in him the tendency in his next incarnation to experience some obstacle in his own body and, by overcoming this, he will be in the position to compensate for certain actions in his previous life. There is one illness in particular, known to us today as diphtheria, which frequently appears when there is a karmic complication of this kind due to a life-style dominated by emotions and passions in a previous existence.

We will deal with the causes of illness at greater length in the course of these lectures. But first of all we need to take an even closer look at some of the fundamental principles involved to find an answer to this question: Why is it that a person enters into existence through birth – equipped through his karma with the tendency to achieve certain things by overcoming a particular illness. Why is it that he should manage in one case to overcome the illness and acquire strengths to help him develop further, while in another he succumbs to the illness?

The fact that we are able to fall ill at all, actually to seek illness because of our karma, is connected with certain principles which we have often discussed already in our anthroposophical studies. We know that the luciferic forces entered human development at a certain point of the earth's evolution. These are connected to beings which remained behind during the ancient Moon evolution and did not attain, as it were, the normal stage of development on earth. Owing to this, something emanating from these luciferic beings was implanted into man's astral body before his 'I' was activated. So the influence of these beings was once exercised on man's astral body, and he has retained it throughout his evolution. This luciferic influence plays a part in human evolution; but for our present task it is important to point out that through the luciferic forces within him the human being was imbued with something suited to tempt him to be less good than he would have been without the luciferic influence. It also gave him the tendency to act and judge more from his emotions, passions and desires than he would have done if the luciferic influence had not entered. This influence produced a change in the real human individuality which became more subject to what we may call the world of drives and passions than would other-wise have been the case, and it is because of this influence that the human being has become much more identified with the physical earthly world than he would otherwise have been. Through the luciferic influence the human being has entered more into his body and has identified himself more with it, for if the influence of the luciferic beings had not been there, many of the things that allure human beings to desire certain things would not have arisen. Human beings would have been quite indifferent to these allurements. But allurements of the external world of the senses came through this influence of Lucifer, and human beings yielded to them. The individuality which was given by the 'I' was permeated with the activities proceeding from the luciferic principle, and so it came about that in his first incarnation on earth the human being succumbed to the allurements of the luciferic principle and carried these enticements with him into later lives. We can say that the way in which he succumbed to the allurements of the luciferic principle became an integral part of his karma.

Now, if someone had taken only this principle into himself he would have succumbed more and more to the allurements of the earthly world; he would gradually have been obliged to resign the prospect of breaking loose again from this world. We know that the Christ influence which came later counteracted the luciferic principle and balanced it again, as it were, so that in the course of evolution the human being again received the means by which to rid himself of the luciferic influence. But with this influence something else was given at the same time. The fact that this influence had penetrated into the human being's astral body made the whole of the external world into which he entered appear different to him. Lucifer entered into the inner being of man, who then saw the world around him through Lucifer. His vision of the earthly world was thereby clouded and his external impressions were mingled with what we call the ahrimanic influence.[3] Ahriman could only insinuate himself and make the external world into illusion because we had previously created from within the tendency towards illusion and maya. Thus the ahrimanic influence which came into the external world was a consequence of the luciferic influence. One could say that when once the luciferic forces were there, the human being enmeshed himself more in the sense-world than he would have done without this influence; but in that he also created the possibility to absorb the ahrimanic influence with every external perception. Thus in the human individuality which goes through incarnations on the earth there is a luciferic influence and, as a result of this, the ahrimanic influence. These two powers are continually fighting in the human individuality which has become their field of battle.

Man in his ordinary consciousness is still exposed to the allurements of Lucifer which work from the passions and emotions of his astral body; also he is subject to the entice-ments of Ahriman which come to him from outside in the way of error, deception, and so forth, in regard to the outer world. Therefore, as long as a person is incarnated on the earth with his mental images forming barriers, so that the influence of Lucifer and Ahriman cannot penetrate deeper but is hindered by these mental images or ideas, his acts will be guided by his moral or intellectual judgement. When a person between birth and death sins against morality in following Lucifer, or against logic or sound thinking in following Ahriman, that concerns only his ordinary conscious soul life. When, on the other hand, he passes through the portal of death, the life of idea which is bound to the instrument of the brain ceases, and a different form of consciousness begins. Then all the things which in the life between birth and death are subject to a person's moral or rational judgement penetrate down into the foundation of the human being, into that which, after kamaloca, organizes the next existence and imprints itself into the formative forces, which then construct a threefold human body. Errors resulting from devotion to Ahriman develop into forces of disease which affect man through his etheric body, whereas misdemeanours which are subject to one's moral judgement in life develop into causes of disease which tend to originate in the astral body.

From this we see how, in fact, our errors from the ahrimanic forces within us, including such conscious errors as lies, and so on, develop into causes of disease, if we do not merely consider the one incarnation but observe the effect of one incarnation on the next. We see also how the luciferic influences in the same way become the causes of disease, and we may in fact say that our errors do not go unpunished. We bear the stamp of our errors in our next incarnation. But we do this from a higher reason than that of our ordinary consciousness – from a consciousness which during the period between death and a new birth directs us to make ourselves so strong that we shall no longer be exposed to these temptations. Thus in our life disease even plays the part of a great teacher. If we study illnesses in this way we shall see unmistakably that an illness is a manifestation of either luciferic or ahrimanic influences. When these things are understood by those who will practise healing according to the principles of spiritual science their influence on the human organism will be infinitely more profound than it can be today.

We can examine certain forms of disease from this standpoint. Let us take pneumonia, for example; it is a karmic effect which follows when during his life in kamaloca the person in question looks back to a character which had within it the tendency towards sexual excess, and a desire to live a sensual life. Do not confuse what is now ascribed to a previous consciousness with what appears in the consciousness in the following incarnation. This is quite a different matter. Indeed, that which a person sees during his life in kamaloca will so transform itself that forces are imprinted in him by means of which he will overcome pneumonia. For it is exactly in the overcoming of this disease, in the self-healing which is then striven for, that the human individuality acts in opposition to the luciferic powers and wages a pitched battle against them. Therefore in the overcoming of pneumonia the opportunity is given to lay aside that which was a defect in the character in a previous incarnation. In this complaint we see unmistakably our battle against the luciferic powers.

The case is different in the so-called 'tuberculosis of the lungs', when we see the singular phenomenon whereby the self-healing forces become active and the harmful influences which arise are surrounded, encompassed, as it were, by something like connective tissue; this is then filled in with calcareous substance which forms solid inclusions. It is quite possible to have such inclusions in one's lungs; in fact it is a lot more common than one would think. This phenomenon always points to a tubercular lung that has been healed. Where such a thing has taken place, a war has been waged by the human inner being against what the ahrimanic forces have produced. It is a defensive process from within against what has been brought about by external materiality, in order to lead to the independence of the human being in this special sense.

We have shown how, in fact, the two principles – the ahrimanic and the luciferic – are at work at the very foundation of a disease. And in many ways it can be pointed out that in the various forms of disease one distinguishes essentially two types, the ahrimanic and the luciferic. If this were considered, the true principles would be discovered by which to find a suitable remedy for the patient; for luciferic diseases will require entirely different remedies from the ahrimanic.

Today external forces are used for the purposes of healing in a way which betrays a certain want of judgement – forces such as electro-therapy, the cold water treatment, and so on. Much light could be thrown by spiritual science on the suitability of one method or another, if it were first decided whether a luciferic or ahrimanic illness is being treated. For example, electro-therapy ought not to be used in illnesses which originate from luciferic causes, but only in ahrimanic forms of illness. For electricity, which has no connection whatever with the activities of Lucifer, is useless in treating luciferic forms of disease; it belongs to the sphere of the ahrimanic beings, although, of course, other beings beside the ahrimanic make use of the forces of electricity. On the other hand, heat and cold belong to the sphere of Lucifer. Everything which has to do with making the human body warmer or colder, or that which makes it warmer or colder through external influences, belongs to the sphere of Lucifer; and in all the cases in which we have to deal with heat or cold we have a type of luciferic form of disease.

From this we see how karma works in illness and how it works to overcome illness. It will now no longer seem incomprehensible that in karma there also lies the curability or incurability of a disease. If we clearly understand that the aim – the karmic aim – of illness is the progress and the improvement of man, we must presume that if a person in accordance with the wisdom which he brings with him into this existence from the kamaloca period contracts a disease, he then develops the healing forces which involve a strengthening of his inner forces and the possibility of rising higher. Let us suppose that a person in the life before him, owing to his general constitution and his remaining karma, were to have the force of progressing during this life by means of that which he has acquired through illness. Then the healing has an object. The person comes forth healed from the illness, having gained what he was to gain. Through the conquest of the illness he has acquired perfect forces where previously he had imperfect forces. If through his karma he is equipped with such powers, and if through the favourable circumstances of his former destiny he is so placed in the world that he can use the new forces, and can work so as to be of use to himself and others, then healing comes about and he will find a way out of the illness.

Now let us suppose a case in which a person overcomes a disease, develops the healing forces, and then is confronted with a life which exacts from him a degree of perfection he has not yet gained. He would, indeed, gain something through the conquered disease, but for other karmic reasons he would not have gained enough to assist others. Then his deeper subconscious says: 'Here you have no opportunity of receiving the full force of what you really ought to have. You had to go into this incarnation to gain the degree of perfection which you can only attain in the physical body by overcoming the disease. That you had to acquire; but you cannot develop it further. You have now to go into conditions in which your physical body and the other forces do not disturb you, where you can freely work out what you have gained through the illness.' Such an individual seeks for death so as to use further, between death and another birth, what he cannot use in life. Such a soul goes through the phase between death and a new birth in order to construct an organization with the stronger forces it has gained by overcoming disease. In this way, through the presence of an illness, a payment on account, as it were, may be made, and the payment is completed after passing through death.

When we consider the question in this way we cannot but recognize that there appear to be karmic reasons for the fact that some illnesses can be cured whilst others end in death.

Looking at illness in this way will enable us to feel reconciled with life, as it were, in a very real sense, through the higher point of view engendered by this sense of karma; for we will know that the law of karma provides for the development of the human being even when an illness ends in death; even then, the illness's purpose is to support the individual's development to a greater state of perfection. Now, it would be inadmissible to conclude from this that there might be cases where one ought veritably to wish for a certain illness to end in death. It would be inadmissible for anyone to say such a thing because the decision whether an illness is to be cured or not is subject to a higher kind of reason than that encompassed by our normal consciousness. In the world between birth and death, and with our ordinary consciousness, we must humbly desist from attempting to decide such questions. However, with our higher consciousness we may by all means adopt a point of view from which we are able to accept even death as a gift from the higher spiritual powers. But we must not presume to occupy such a higher point of view with that consciousness which is given us to help and work in the world. We might easily succumb to error and would then interfere terribly in something in which we must not ever interfere: the sphere of human freedom. If we can help a person to develop the self-healing forces, or support the work of nature ourselves, so that a cure may come about, we must do it. And if the question should arise as to whether the patient ought to live on further, or whether he would be more helped if he died, our assistance must nevertheless always be given towards healing. If this is done we help the human individuality to use its own powers, and the medical assistance only supports him in this. Then it will not interfere with the human individuality. It would be quite different if we were to help someone suffering from an incurable illness to seek his further progress in another world. We should then interfere with his individuality and deliver it up to another sphere of influence. We should be imposing our will upon the other. Such decisions must be left to the individual concerned. In other words, we must do everything possible for him to be cured, for all the deliberations concerning healing must come from the consciousness which is appropriate for our earth, or else we should reach beyond our earth sphere, where entirely different forces come into play.

Thus we see that a true karmic understanding concerning the curability and incurability of disease leads to our doing everything possible to help the person who is ill, and, on the other hand, helps us to accept with equanimity when a different decision comes from another sphere. This is all we need to do when we are confronted with such decisions. We need to find a point of view from which the incurability of a disease does not depress us, as though the world contained only what is imperfect and evil. Our insights into karma must never inhibit our will to heal. In fact, our understanding of karma will reconcile us to the hardest of destinies.

Thus we have seen today how the understanding of karma alone makes it possible for us to comprehend the course of an illness in the right way, and to understand that in our present life we see the karmic effects of our previous life. Detailed examples will be given in the course of our next discussions.

We will now have to study the difference between two special forms of illness – those which come from our inner being and strike us rather more obviously as karmically caused, and those other forms of illness that appear to hit us by chance, through exposure to injuries from outside or involvement in some event or other. How can we extend our understanding of karma to encompass even things like falling under a train, for instance?[4] How can we grasp so-called 'chance' illnesses in terms of karma?

LECTURE 5

Karma in Relation to Natural and Accidental Illness

Hamburg, 20 May 1910

What I said in yesterday's lecture is of fundamental importance to what we are going to deal with today. Therefore I would like to recapitulate the main points.

We began by saying that views concerning cures and medicines have in the course of a relatively short time, during the last century, undergone a radical change. And we pointed to the fact that in the sixteenth and seventeenth centuries that view was developed which was based entirely upon the theory that for every illness which was given a name, and which it was believed could be strictly defined, some remedy must exist upon earth. And it was firmly believed that by the use of the remedy in question the course of the illness must be influenced. We then pointed out that this view prevailed more or less until the nineteenth century, and side by side with this we showed the complete reversal of this opinion which found expression chiefly in the nihilism of the Viennese school, founded by the famous physician Dietl, and carried on by Skoda and some of his pupils. We characterized the nihilistic current of thought by saying that it not merely harboured doubts as to the existence of any absolute connection between one remedy or another, one manipulation or another in respect to the treatment of illness and the illness itself, but would no longer concern itself with any such connection. The idea of so-called 'self-healing' penetrated the minds of the young doctors influenced by this school. Skoda himself made the following significant statement to this school: 'We may be able to diagnose an illness, to explain, and perhaps also to describe it, but remedy for it we have none.' This point of view originated from the proofs furnished by Dietl to the effect that, given the necessary conditions, an illness such as pneumonia will, with temporizing treatment, take such a course as to develop self-healing forces at the end of a certain period. By means of statistics he was able to prove that a temporizing treatment showed neither fewer cures nor more deaths than the remedies ordinarily in use. At that time the term 'therapeutic nihilism' was not without justification, for it is quite true that the doctors of this school were powerless against the patient's conviction that there simply must exist a remedy, a prescription. The patient would not yield, nor would his friends. A remedy had to be prescribed, and the followers of this school got out of the difficulty by prescribing a thin solution of gum arabic which, according to their opinion, would have the same effect as the remedies previously in use. From this we have learnt how the modern scientific world is moving in the direction of what one might call the karmic connections of life. For now they had to find an answer to the question: 'How is that which we may call "self-healing" brought about? Or better, why does it take place? And why in some cases can there be no self-healing or cure of any kind?'

The fact that an entire school led by eminent authorities in the field of medicine thought of introducing the concept of self-healing should have made anyone who thinks this over conclude that there must be something in the course of an illness which contributes to overcoming it! And this would have had to lead to further inquiries concerning the more hidden causes of illness. I have now tried to demonstrate how such karmic reasons for illness in human life might be found. I pointed out that what we do or feel in the normal course of life, whether good or bad, wise or unwise, right or wrong, does not really penetrate into the deeper layers of our organism. And I have told you why things which relate to our moral or intellectual judgement or our feelings remain at the surface, and are not subject to that law which we also discussed, which works into the deeper layers of our organism. As I have shown, there is a kind of barrier which prevents immorality from entering into the deeper forces of the human organism. What we do between birth and death is accompanied by the mental images or ideas we form in our consciousness, and this forms a defence against our deeds and thoughts interfering with the forces of our organism. The conscious mental images which accompany what we do or otherwise experience provide a protective barrier which prevents the results of our actions from affecting our organism.

I also referred to the importance of experiences that have been forgotten and cannot be retrieved – experiences which we cannot recall to consciousness. Such experiences do penetrate into our inner organism in a certain way, and they can affect its formative forces, as the protective barrier formed by mental images is lacking in this case. And I also pointed to those forms of illness which are even closer to the surface, such as neurosis, neurasthenia, and so forth. A light is thrown even upon hysterical conditions. As we said, the cause of such conditions must be sought for in the ideas or mental images that have been forgotten, which have fallen out of the complex of consciousness and have sunk down into the inner soul-life where, as a sort of wedge, they assert themselves in the form of disease. We further pointed out the tremendous significance of the period which lies between birth and the time when we first begin to remember our experiences; and our attention was drawn to the fact that what at an earlier stage has been forgotten, continues to be active within our living organism, forming, as it were, an alliance with the deeper forces of our organism, and thereby influencing our organism itself. As we see, a whole complex of mental images, a number of experiences, must sink down into the deeper foundations of our being before they can intervene in our organism. I then pointed out that this sinking down is most thorough when we have passed through the gate of death and are experiencing the further existence between death and a new birth. The quality of all experiences is then transformed into forces which now develop an organizing activity, and the feelings which we have experienced during the period between death and a new birth will become part of the formative forces that take part in the rebuilding of the body when we return to a new life. In these formative forces man now carries within him the result of what at an earlier stage he held within his soul-life, perhaps even in his conscious life of ideas. And further we could point to the fact that man with his conscious conceptions permeated by the 'I' oscillates between two influences present in the world – between the luciferic and the ahrimanic influences. When, owing to the characteristics of our astral body, we have done wrong through violent emotions, temper, and so forth, we are driven thereto by luciferic forces. If such deeds then take the course we have just now described, if they are transformed into formative forces, they will be dwelling as causes of luciferic disease within the formative forces, and will lay the foundations of our new body. We have further seen that we are subject also to the ahrimanic forces which affect us more from outside. And again we had to admit, concerning the ahrimanic forces, that they are transformed into formative forces, into forces shaping the newly built organism when man enters existence through birth, and in so far as the ahrimanic influences mingle with the formative forces, so far as we may speak of ahrimanic predisposition to disease. We then pointed out in detail how the forces act that are developed in this way. I quoted some radical examples of this activity, because in radical examples the picture is more distinct, more clearly defined. I gave the instance of a person who in his previous life had at all times acted in such a way as to produce a weak 'I'-consciousness, and weak self-reliance, and whose 'I' attached little value to itself, becoming absorbed only in generalities and so forth. Such a person will after death develop the tendency to absorb forces that will render him capable of strengthening and perfecting his 'I' in the further incarnation. As a result of this he will seek conditions that will give him an opportunity to fight against certain resistances, so that his weak 'I'-consciousness might be strengthened through resistance. Such a tendency will lead him to seek an opportunity to contract cholera, because in this he will face something that offers an opportunity to conquer those resistances, in the conquest of which he will be led in his next incarnation, or even, should a cure be effected in this same incarnation, to a stronger 'I'-consciousness or to forces which will by way of self-education lead him gradually to a stronger 'I'-consciousness. We have further stated that an illness such as malaria affords an opportunity to compensate for the overbearing 'I'-consciousness which has been engendered by the soul in an earlier life through its deeds and emotions.

Those of us who took part in our earlier anthroposophical studies will understand such a course of events. It has always been said that man's 'I' finds its physical expression in his blood. Both of these illnesses which have just been mentioned are connected with blood and the laws of blood. They are so connected that in the case of cholera there is a thickening of the blood which can be regarded as the 'resistance' which a weak self-reliance must experience, and by means of which it is trying to develop. We shall also be able to understand that in a case of malaria we are faced with an impoverishment of the blood, and that an over-developed 'I'-consciousness needs the opportunity of being led to an impossible extreme. This impoverishment of the blood of an over-developed 'I' will result in all efforts ending in annihilation. Naturally these things are extremely intimately connected within the human organism, but if you examine them, you will soon find them comprehensible.

From all of this we understand the following: When we are dealing with an organism formed by a soul that has brought with it the tendency to overcome some imperfection in one or another direction, the person concerned will tend to become impregnated with a predisposition to a certain illness, but at the same time he will have the capacity of fighting this illness which is produced for no other reason than to provide the means of a cure. And a cure will be effected when the person, in accordance with his whole karma, acquires through the conquest of the illness such forces as will enable him through the rest of his life to make true progress by means of his work on the physical plane. In other words, if the stimulating forces are so strong that the individual concerned is able to acquire upon the physical plane itself those qualities, on account of which the illness broke out, then he will be able to work with that reinforced power which he lacked before, and which he gained from the healing process. But if his overall karma is such that he did indeed intend to construct his organism so that through the conquest of the illness in question it should acquire forces which lead nearer to perfection, and yet because of the complexity of the causes was forced to leave his organism weak in another direction, then it may be that, although the forces which are developed and applied in the healing process strengthen him, they do not do so sufficiently to make the individual concerned equal to his work upon the physical plane. In a case like this the person – unable to use his newly acquired powers on the physical plane – will utilize them when he passes through the gate of death. He will attempt to supplement his powers by what he could not produce on the physical plane. At his next incarnation these powers will be manifested in the configuration of his body.

Bearing this in mind, one more indication should be given in relation to those forms of illness leading neither to a real cure nor to death but to chronic conditions, to a kind of languishing state. It is extremely important indeed to under-stand what happens in the case of chronic illness. It may be the case that whatever healing could be effected, with regard to the way in which the various bodies relate to one another, has indeed been achieved; the illness has been overcome in a certain sense. But in another sense it might not have been overcome. In other words, etheric and physical bodies may have been harmonized, whilst the imbalance between etheric body and astral body continues to exist. As a result the individual in question oscillates between endeavouring to heal and not being able to heal. In a case like that it is of the utmost importance for the affected individual to make the best possible use of whatever actual healing has already been achieved. Yet it is what happens least of all in reality, for it is precisely in the case of those illnesses that become chronic that we find ourselves in a vicious circle. If we were able in a case like that to isolate that part of our organism that has achieved a certain cure, if we could let it be, as it were, and withdraw from the healthy part the rest which is still in disturbance and disorder – which is usually rooted in the astral body – we would do ourselves a great favour. But many things oppose this, and chiefly the fact that when we have had an illness resulting in a chronic condition, we are living all the time under the influence of that condition, and, if I may thus crudely express myself, we can never really completely forget our condition, never really arrive at a withdrawing of that which is not yet healthy, so as to treat it by itself. On the contrary, through thinking continually about the sickly part of our organism, we bring, as it were, our healthy part into some kind of relationship with the sickness and thus irritate it anew.

This is a special process, and in order to make it clearer I should like to explain the facts of the matter in terms of spiritual science and tell you what can be perceived clairvoyantly when a person has gone through an illness, and has retained something which may be termed chronic. The same applies, by the way, when there is no apparent acute illness, but when a chronic disease is developed without any acute state having been specially noticed. In most of these cases it is possible to see that there is an unstable state of balance between the etheric and the physical body, an oscillation of the forces which is not normal, but can be lived with. This oscillation of forces which appertain to the etheric body and the physical body bring about a continual state of irritation in the individual concerned, which leads to continuous states of agitation. Clairvoyant consciousness sees this agitation transmitted to the astral body, and these states of excitability continually force their way into that part of the organism which is partly ill and partly well, which results in instability as opposed to balance. These states of astral agitation result in a marked deterioration of the individual's general state of health, which would otherwise be far better.

Please consider that in this context the astral does not relate to the person's consciousness, but rather to inner states of soul agitation, of which the patient is not aware to the extent of being willing to admit to them. As the barrier provided by mental images is non-existent in such cases, these emotional states of upheaval, these continuous states of weariness and inner discontent, will not always work as conscious forces, but rather as the organizing or life forces. Seated within our deeper being they continually irritate that part which is partly healthy and partly sick. If the patient by means of a strong discipline of the soul could forget his condition for some time at least, he would gain such satisfaction from this, that even from this satisfaction itself he could derive the necessary strength to carry on further. If he could forget his state completely and develop the strong will to say: 'I will not bother with my condition now!' – and if he would then apply the soul forces released in that manner to something spiritual, that would elevate him and inwardly satisfy his soul. If he liberated the forces that are continuously occupied with the sensation of aches and pains, oppression and so on, he would gain great satisfaction. For if we do not live through these feelings, the forces are free, and they are at our disposal.

Naturally it will not be of much use merely to say we don't want to take notice of these aches and pains, for if we do not put these liberated forces to spiritual use, the former conditions will soon return. If, however, we employ these liberated forces for a spiritual purpose which will absorb the soul, we shall soon discover that we are attaining in a complicated way that which our organism would otherwise have attained without our assistance through the conquest of the illness.

Naturally the person in question would have to be careful not to fill his soul with something directly connected with his illness. For instance, if someone suffering from a weakness of the eyes were to read a great deal so as to avoid thinking of this, he would naturally not arrive at his goal. But it is quite unnecessary to resort to further illustrations. We have all noticed how useful it is when we are slightly indisposed to be able to forget that indisposition, especially if we gain this forgetfulness by occupying ourselves with something different. Such is a positive and wholesome forgetfulness. This already suggests to us that we are not entirely impotent in the face of the karmic effects of those transgressions of our earlier lives which are expressed in the form of illness. After all, if we recognize that everything which is subject to moral, emotional and intellectual judgement during our life between birth and death cannot penetrate so deeply during one single life as to become the cause of an organic disease, but that in the period between death and a new birth it may penetrate so deeply into the human essence as to cause disease, we must allow for the fact that it should be possible to re-transform these processes into conscious processes.

The question might be put thus: If illnesses are the karmic results of spiritual or other events called forth or experienced by the soul, if they are the metamorphosis of such causes, is it not conceivable then – in fact, is it not borne out by the spiritual facts – that the product of the metamorphosis, namely, the illness, might be avoided? Might it not be avoided if we could substitute the process of healing, that which is drawn from the organs in the form of illness to educate us, with its spiritual counterpart, its spiritual equivalent? Should we not thus, if we were sufficiently wise, transform illness into a spiritual process and accomplish through our soul forces the self-education that would otherwise be accomplished through illness?

The feasibility of this may be demonstrated by an example. Here again we must insist that only those examples are given which have been investigated by spiritual science. They are not hypothetical assertions but actual 'cases'. A certain person contracts measles in later life, and we seek for the karmic connection in this case. We find that this case of measles appeared as the karmic effect of occurrences in a preceding life – occurrences such as these: In a preceding life the individuality in question disliked concerning himself with the external world but occupied himself a great deal with himself, though not in the ordinary egotistical sense. He investigated much, meditated much, though not with regard to the facts of the external world, but with a strong concentration on his inner life of soul. We meet many people today, too, who believe that through self-concentration and through brooding within themselves, they will arrive at the solution of world riddles. The person in question sought to cope with his life by constantly pondering over how to conduct himself in different situations. The weakness of soul resulting from this led to the formation of forces during his existence between death and a new birth which exposed his organism to an attack of measles comparatively late in life.

We might now ask: 'If on the one hand we have the attack of measles which is the physical karmic effect of an earlier life, how is it then with the soul?' For the earlier life will also karmically produce a certain condition of the soul.

The soul condition will prove itself to be such that the personality in question, during the life in which the attack of measles took place, was again and again subject to self-deception. Thus in the self-deception we must see the psychic karmic result of this earlier life, and the attack of measles the physical karmic result.

Let us now assume that this personality, before developing measles, had succeeded in gaining such soul forces that he was no longer exposed to all kinds of self-deception, having completely corrected this failing. In this case the acquired soul force would have rendered the attack of measles quite unnecessary, since the tendencies brought forth in this organism during its formation had been effaced through the stronger soul forces acquired by self-education. Of course, I cannot talk to you ad infinitum about these things; but if you really examined what goes on in life around you and considered every single detail from the point of view I have just described, you would invariably find that outer facts bear out fully what I have related to you – to the minutest detail. And what I have said about a case of measles can lead to an explanation why measles is one of the illnesses of childhood. For the failings I have mentioned are present in a great many lives and especially in certain periods they prevailed in many lives. When such a personality enters existence he will be anxious to make the corresponding correction as soon as possible. In the period between birth and the general appearance of children's complaints which effect an organic self-education, there can as a rule be no question of any education of the soul.

From this we see that in a certain respect we can really speak of illness being transformed back into a spiritual process. And it is most significant that when this process has entered the soul as a life principle, it will evoke an inner disposition which has a healing effect upon the soul. We need not be surprised that in our time we are able to influence the soul so little. Anyone who is able to evaluate our present period from the standpoint of spiritual science will understand why so many medical people, so many doctors, become materialists, in other words, why they despair of any effects of the soul whatsoever. For most people never occupy themselves with anything which has vital force. All the stuff produced today is devoid of vital force for the soul. That is why anyone wishing to work for spiritual science feels in this anthroposphical activity something extremely wholesome, for spiritual science can again bring to mankind something which enters the soul so that it is drawn away from what was formed in the physical organism. But we must not confuse what appears at the beginning of such a movement as anthroposophy with what this movement can be in reality. After all, many of the misconceptions rampant in the world outside are brought right into the anthroposophical movement, because people, on becoming anthroposophists, often bring to anthroposophy exactly the same interests they have for other things, and also all the bad habits they have outside. In that way much of the degeneracy of our age is brought in. Yet, when some such degeneracy appears in the people in question, the world says that this is the effect of anthroposophy. That is, of course, a very cheap statement.

I have shown you now how the karmic thread runs from one incarnation to the next, but this is only one aspect of the overall reality. If you develop a sense of how karma works from incarnation to incarnation, you will want to know a lot more. Many more aspects will be explored in the course of these lectures, but first of all we must deal with the question: What difference is there between an illness due to external causes and an illness where the cause lies exclusively in the human organism itself? We are tempted to dispose of the latter illnesses by saying that they come of their own accord without any external provocation. But this is not so. In a certain sense we are justified in saying that there are illnesses to which we are particularly prone on account of our inner organism. A great many forms of illness, however, we shall be able to trace to external causes; not indeed everything that happens to us, but much that befalls us from outside. If we break a leg, for instance, we are obliged to account for it by external causes. We must also include within external causes the effects of the weather, and numerous cases of disease caused by bad inner city housing. Here again we envisage a wide field. An experienced person looking on the world will find it easy to explain why the modern trend of the medical profession is to seek the causes of illness in external influences, and especially in germs. Of these, a witty gentleman said, not without justification: 'Today it is said that illnesses are caused by germs, just as it was formerly said that they came from God, the devil, and so forth. In the thirteenth century it was said that illnesses came from God; in the fifteenth it was said that they came from the devil; later it was said that illnesses came from the humours; today we say that illnesses come from germs!'[1] These are the views that superseded one another in the course of time.

Thus we speak of external causes of human illness or health. In this context modern man is easily tempted to employ a word that is eminently suited to confuse one's thinking about the way the world is arranged. When someone who previously enjoyed good health moves into an area where there is an epidemic of diphtheria or influenza, and subsequently falls ill, modern man would certainly be inclined to say that the person concerned contracted the germs causing the illness as a result of moving into that area, and he will probably use the word 'chance' in this context. There is a general tendency to speak of accidental influences or chance events. In actual fact chance is a problematic term whatever one's world view may be. And as long as we don't even attempt to make clear in some way what actually is so conveniently referred to as 'chance', we cannot hope to advance to any reasonably satisfactory view of the world. This is the starting point of the theme 'Natural illnesses and accidental illnesses in human life'. It is essential that we should first of all try to throw some light on the word chance.

Is not chance itself something which ought to make us suspicious of the way it is generally conceived of today? I already referred on a previous occasion to what a certain educated gentleman in the eighteenth century said in relation to the custom of erecting monuments to great explorers, inventors and such like;[2] he said – not without justification – that most monuments by far ought to be erected to 'chance' if one really followed the course of history objectively! Is it not strange that if we take a closer look at historical development we can make peculiar discoveries about what chance often conceals. As I have mentioned before, we owe the telescope to the fact that children were once playing with optical lenses in an optical laboratory. In their play they formed a combination by means of which someone then produced a telescope.

You might also recall the famous lamp in the cathedral of Pisa, which before the time of Galileo was seen by thousands and thousands, oscillating with the same regularity. But it remained for Galileo to find out by experiment how these oscillations coincided with the course of his blood circulation, whereby he discovered the famous laws of the pendulum.[3] Had we not known these, the whole of our culture would have received a very different colouring. Let us try to find a meaning in human evolution, and then see whether we should still wish to maintain that only chance was at work when Galileo made this important discovery. Let us consider yet another case.

We are aware what Luther's translation of the Bible means to the civilized countries of Europe.[4] It profoundly influenced religious sentiment and thought and also the development of what we call the German literary language. I simply mention the fact without comment. I insist only on the profound influence which this translation exercised. We must endeavour to see the significance of that education which, during the course of several centuries, came to mankind as a result of Luther's translation of the Bible. Let us endeavour to perceive a meaning in this, and then let us consider the following fact.

Up to a certain period of his life Luther was deeply imbued with the feeling and desire so to order his life as to become a veritable 'child of God'. This desire had been brought about by a constant reading of the Bible. The custom prevailed among the Augustinian monks of reading preferably the work of the Fathers of the Church, but Luther passed to the spiritual enjoyment of the Bible itself. Thus he was led to this intense feeling of being a 'child of God', and under this influence he fulfilled his duties as teacher of theology in the first Wittenberg period. The fact that I should now like to emphasize is that Luther had a certain reluctance to acquiring the title of Doctor of Theology. It was during a chance conversation with an old friend of the Erfurt Augustinian monastery that he was persuaded to try for the doctorate. For this purpose he needed to resume and step up his studies of the Bible. Thus it was the chance conversation with his friend which led to a renewed study of the Bible, and to all that resulted from it.

Try to conceive from the point of view of the last centuries the significance of the 'chance' that Luther once conversed with that friend and was persuaded to try for the doctorate in theology. You will be obliged to see that it would be grotesque to connect this human evolution with a 'chance' event.

From what has been said we shall first of all conclude that perhaps after all there is something more in chance than is usually supposed. As a rule we believe chance to be something which cannot be satisfactorily explained either by the laws of nature or the laws of life, and that it constitutes a kind of surplus over and above what can be explained. Let us now view this against the background of a fact which has helped us to understand so many aspects of life. Man, since he began his earth existence, has been subject to the two forces of the luciferic and ahrimanic principles. These forces and principles continually penetrate into the human being. While the luciferic forces act more within by influencing our astral body, the ahrimanic forces act rather through the external impressions which we receive. In what we receive from the external world there are contained the ahrimanic forces, and in what arises and acts within the soul in the form of joy and dejection, desires, and so forth, there are contained the luciferic forces. The luciferic as well as the ahrimanic principles induce us to give way to error. The luciferic principle induces us to deceive ourselves as to our own inner life, to judge our inner life wrongly, to see maya, illusion within ourselves.

If we contemplate life rationally, we shall not find it difficult to discover maya in our own soul life. Let us consider how very often we persuade ourselves that we have done one thing or another for this or that reason. Generally the reason is quite a different one, and far more profound. It may be found in temper, desire, or passion, but in our superficial consciousness we give quite a different explanation. We try especially hard to deny things which are not generally approved of and, when we are driven to some act from purely egotistical motives, we frequently find ourselves clothing these crude egotistical impulses with a cloak of unselfishness, and explaining why it was necessary for us to act in this way.

However, normally we are not aware that we act like this. When we become aware of it, there generally begins an improvement accompanied by a certain feeling of shame. The worst of it is that for the most part we are ignorant of the fact that we are driven to something from the depths of our soul – and then we invent a motive for the deed in question. This has also been discovered by modern psychologists. Yet, because today's education in psychology is so scanty, the materialist psychologists of our time come up with such grotesque misrepresentations of facts like the ones described. They arrive at very peculiar interpretations of life.

If you apply the methods of spiritual research to such matters you will naturally understand their true meaning and characterize the whole phenomenon as follows: There are indeed two influences acting together, namely, our consciousness, and that which dwells in the deeper layers beneath the threshold of consciousness. But when the same facts are observed by a materialistic psychologist, he will set to work differently. He will immediately fabricate a theory about the difference between the pretext we presume for our deeds and the real motive. If, for instance, a psychologist discusses the suicides of schoolchildren which occur so frequently nowadays, he will say that what is quoted as pretext is not the real motive; that the real motive lies far deeper, being found mostly in a misdirected sexual life, and that the real motive is so transformed that it deludes the consciousness for some reason or other.

Often this may be so, but anyone with the slightest insight into the true depths of psychology would never construct a comprehensive theory out of that. Such a theory could easily be refuted, for if the case really is such that pretext is nothing, and motive everything, this would also apply to the psychologist himself, and we should be forced to say that with him, too, what he is telling us and developing as a theory is but a pretext. If we were to search for deeper reasons, perhaps the reasons alleged by him would be found to be of exactly the same nature. If such a psychologist had really fully grasped the impossibility of a judgement based on a conclusion such as: 'All idiots are liars', and furthermore that such a judgement is lop-sided when uttered by an idiot; if he had really grasped the reason why this is so he would have also learnt what peculiar vicious circles are created when in certain fields assertions can be turned back on the one making them. Yet there is extraordinarily little real in-depth education in nearly all our literature. Hence people generally do not notice anymore what they are doing. Therefore it will be essential for spiritual science in particular to avoid such logical confusion in all respects. These logical confusions are least avoided by modern philosophers dealing with the science of the soul. And our example is a very typical one. It exemplifies the kinds of trick luciferic forces play upon us, turning our entire soul-life into *maya*, so that we can deceive ourselves about the real motives for our deeds instead of recognizing what dwells within us.

In this realm it is important to acquire a stricter self-discipline. Today words are as a rule handled with great facility. A word, however, can lead to great error and confusion. The word has but to have a pleasing sound, and it creates the impression of a charitable deed. Even the pleasant sound of a sentence will betray us into believing that the motive in question is within our soul, while in truth the egotistical principle may be concealed behind it without our being aware of its presence, because we have not the will to arrive at true self-knowledge. Thus we see Lucifer active on the one side. How does Ahriman act on the other?

Ahriman is that principle which intermingles with our perceptions and enters us from outside. Ahriman's activity is strongest when we feel: 'Thinking is not taking me any further; I have reached a critical point in my thinking, it is caught up in a great knot.' Then the ahrimanic principle seizes the occasion to penetrate us as through a rift in the external world. If we follow the course of world events and the more obvious occurrences, if, for instance, we pursue modern physics back to the moment when Galileo was sitting in front of the oscillating church lamp in the cathedral of Pisa, we can spin a thought-net embracing all these events whereby the matter will be easily explained. Everything will be quite clear, but the moment we arrive at the oscillating church lamp our thoughts become confused. That is the window through which the ahrimanic forces penetrate us with the greatest strength, and that is where our thought refuses to grasp that very thing in the phenomena that can bring reason and understanding into the matter. Here is also what we call 'chance'. It is here that Ahriman becomes most dangerous to us. The very phenomena we call 'chance' are those by which we are most easily deluded by Ahriman.

Thus we shall learn to understand that it is not the nature of facts themselves that induces us to speak of 'chance', but that it depends on ourselves and our own development. Little by little we shall have to educate ourselves to penetrate *maya* and illusion, that is to say, we must gain insight into matters where Ahriman's influence is at its strongest. And especially in the context of major causes of illness, and the light that is to be shed over the course of many an illness, we will have to approach the phenomena from this point of view. First of all we shall have to try and understand to what extent it is not a matter of chance that someone should be travelling on the very train on which he may lose his life, or that someone at a definite period should be exposed to disease-germs affecting him from outside, or to some other cause of illness. Once we are capable of researching such matters with heightened understanding we will grasp the real nature and significance of illness on an even deeper level.

Today I had to show in somewhat greater detail how Lucifer leads to illusions within ourselves, and how Ahriman becomes intertwined with external perceptions and there leads to *maya*; that it is the work of Lucifer when we delude ourselves with a false motive, and how wrong conclusions in relation to the world of phenomena – Ahriman's deception – lead us to believe in chance. I had to give you this background before demonstrating the working of karma, of the results of an earlier life, in human life even where seemingly accidental outer reasons bring about illness.

LECTURE 6

Karma in Relation to Accidents

Hamburg, 21 May 1910

It is easily understood that karmic law can operate when, in the sense demonstrated, a cause of illness asserts itself from within the human being. But it is more difficult to understand that the experiences and actions of a previous life brought in by the individual at birth can provoke illnesses coming from outside in a certain sense – such illnesses as science calls infections. Nevertheless, if we go deeper into the true nature of karma, we shall learn not merely to understand how these external causes can be related to the experiences and deeds of earlier lives, but we shall also learn that accidents which befall us, events which we are prone to describe as chance, may be closely related to the course of a previous life. We must indeed penetrate somewhat deeper into the whole nature of man's being if we wish to understand the conditions that are so veiled by our human outlook.

We saw yesterday how chance or accident always presents the external event in a veiled form, because in those instances where we speak of chance, the external deceptions created by the ahrimanic powers are the greatest possible. Now let us examine in detail how such accidents, that is to say those events that are generally called 'accidents', come about.

Here it is necessary to bear in mind the law, the truth, the recognition that in life much of what we describe as 'arising from within', or as 'derived from the inner being of man' is already clothed in illusion, because if we truly rise above illusion we find that much of what we at first believe to have originated within man must be described as streaming in from outside. We always encounter this when we have to deal with those dispositions, those traits of character, which are summed up under the name of 'hereditary characteristics'. It seems as though these hereditary characteristics are a part of us only because our forebears had them, and it may appear to us in the most eminent degree as though they had fallen to our lot through no fault of our own, and without our co-operation. It is easy to arrive at a mistaken distinction between what we have brought from earlier incarnations and what we have inherited from our parents and forebears. When we reincarnate we do not come haphazardly to such and such parents or to such and such a country. There are reasons for all of this and these relate to our innermost being. Even in those hereditary characteristics which have nothing to do with illness, we must not assume anything haphazard. In the case of a family such as Bach's,[1] for instance, which produced numerous musicians over many generations – in Bach's family more than twenty more or less gifted musicians were born – one might easily assume a pure line of inheritance, where certain characteristics are inherited and where the individual, due to the presence of these characteristics, develops certain abilities preserved from previous incarnations into musical talent. This is not so, however; the facts are quite different.

Suppose that someone has the opportunity of receiving many musical impressions in a life between birth and death, that these musical impressions passed him by in this life, for the simple reason that he did not have a musical ear. Other impressions which he receives in this life do not pass him by in the same way, because he has organs so formed that he can transform the experiences and impressions into capacities of his own. Here we can say that a person has impressions in the course of his life which are capable of being transformed into capacities and talents through the disposition which he has brought with him from his last birth; and he has other impressions which, on account of his general karma, because he has not received the suitable powers, he cannot transform into the corresponding capacities. They remain, they are stored up, and in the period between death and a new birth they are converted into the particular tendency to be expressed in the next incarnation. And this tendency leads the person to seek for reincarnation in a particular family which can provide him with the suitable organs. Thus if someone has received a great many musical impressions, and was unable to transform them into musical capacities or the ability to enjoy music because of an unmusical ear, it will be this inability which will call forth a tendency in his soul to come into a family where he will inherit a musical ear. From this we shall now see that if a certain family inherits a certain construction of the ear – which can be inherited just as well as the external shape of the nose – all those individuals who in consequence of their former incarnation long for a musical ear, will strive to come into this family. This shows us that, in fact, a person has not inherited a musical ear or a similar gift in a particular incarnation 'by chance', but that he has looked for and actually sought for the inherited characteristic.

If we observe such a person from the moment of his birth, it will seem to us as though the musical sense were within him, a quality of his inner being. If, however, we extend our investigation to the time before his birth, we shall find that the musical ear for which he had to seek is something that has come to him from outside.

Before his birth or conception the musical ear was not

within him. There was only an impulse urging him to acquire such an ear. In this case the person has drawn to himself something external. Before reincarnation the feature which is later termed hereditary was something external. It approached the person, and he hastened to take it. At the moment of incarnation it became internal and made its appearance within. Thus, in speaking of 'hereditary disposition', we suffer from a delusion, because we do not take into account the time when the inner quality was an external one.

Let us now enquire whether what we have just discussed might also apply to external events that occur in our life between birth and death, in other words whether something external could be transformed into something internal. To answer this question we need to go even deeper into the nature of illness and health. I have characterized illness and health from many different angles and you are aware that I refrain from giving definitions but rather try to describe things by building up a picture of their various characteristics by which they may be understood. So let us now expand on this picture by adding some further characteristics.

We must compare sickness and health with something that appears in normal life, namely, sleeping and waking, and we shall then find something of still greater significance. What is taking place within a human being when the daily states of sleeping and waking succeed one another? We know that when we sleep the physical and the etheric bodies are abandoned by the astral body and the 'I', and that awakening represents the return of the astral body and 'I' to the physical and etheric bodies. Every morning on waking, all that constitutes our inner being – astral body and 'I' – dives down again into our physical and etheric bodies. What happens in relation to what we experience on falling asleep and waking up?

If we consider the moment of going to sleep, we see that all experiences which from morning to night fluctuated in our lives, especially the soul experiences of joy and sorrow, happiness and pain, passions, mental images and so forth, sink down into the subconscious. In normal life, when asleep, we ourselves are unconscious. Why do we lose consciousness when we fall asleep? We know that during the state of sleep we are surrounded by a spiritual world, just as in the waking state we are surrounded by the objects and facts of the physical world of the senses. Why do we not perceive this spiritual world? Because in normal life to see the spiritual facts and spiritual things surrounding us at the present stage of human development between going to sleep and awakening would prove dangerous in the highest degree. If the human being today were to pass over consciously into the world which surrounds him between going to sleep and awakening, his astral body, which gained its full development in the ancient Moon period, would flow out into the spiritual world, but this could not be done by the 'I' which can be developed only during the Earth period, and which will have completed its evolution at the end of the Earth period. The 'I' is not sufficiently developed to be able to unfold the whole of its activity between falling asleep and awakening.

If we were to fall asleep consciously, the condition of our 'I' could be illustrated as follows. Let us suppose that we have a small drop of coloured liquid; we drop this into a basin of water and allow it to mix. The colour of that small drop will no more be seen because it has mixed with the whole mass of the water. Something of this nature happens when we leave behind our physical body and etheric body on falling asleep. The latter principles are those which hold together the whole of the human being. As soon as the astral body and 'I' leave the two lower principles, they disperse in all directions, impelled always by this principle of expansion. Thus it would happen that the 'I' would be dissolved, and we should indeed have the pictures of the spiritual world before us, but should not be able to understand them by means of those forces which only the 'I' can bring to bear – the forces of discernment, insight, and so forth – in short, with the consciousness we apply to ordinary life. For the 'I' would be dissolved and we should be frenzied, torn hither and thither, swimming without individuality and without direction in the sea of astral events and impressions. For this reason, because in the case of the normal person the 'I' is not sufficiently strong, it reacts upon the astral body and prevents it from entering consciously the spiritual world which is its true home, until there comes a time when the 'I' will be able to accompany the astral body wherever it may penetrate. Thus there is a good reason for our losing consciousness when we fall asleep, for if it were otherwise, we should not be able to maintain our 'I'. We shall only be able to maintain it sufficiently when our Earth evolution is achieved. That is why we are prevented from unfolding the consciousness of our astral body.

The very reverse takes place when we wake up. When we wake up and sink down into our physical and etheric bodies, we ought in reality to experience their inner nature. But this does not happen, for at the moment of waking up we are prevented from regarding the inner nature of our corporeal being, because our attention is immediately directed to external events. Neither our faculty of sight nor our faculty of perception is directed towards penetration of the inner being, but is distracted by the external world. If we were immediately to apply ourselves to our inner being, there would be an exact reversal of the situation that would occur if we fell asleep and entered the spiritual world with our ordinary consciousness. Everything spiritual that we had acquired through our 'I' in the course of our earth life would then concentrate, and after our re-entry into the physical and etheric bodies it would act upon them most powerfully, bringing about a tremendous increase of our egotism. We should sink down with our 'I'; and all the passions, the desires, the greed, and the egotism of which we are capable would be concentrated within this 'I'. All this egotism would pour away into the life of the senses. To prevent this we are distracted by the external world and barred from penetrating our inner being with our consciousness.

This is also confirmed by the accounts of those mystics who attempted to penetrate the innermost being of man. Consider Meister Eckhart, Johannes Tauler, and other mystics of the Middle Ages,[2] who in order to descend into their own inner being dedicated themselves to a state in which their attention and interest was entirely turned away from the external world. Read the biographies of many saints and mystics who tried to descend into their inner selves. What was their experience? Temptations, tribulations, and similar experiences which they have depicted in vivid colours. This is what emerged from the compressed astral body and 'I' as an opposing force. That is why all those who as mystics have attempted to descend into the inner self found that the further they descended, the more were they impelled to an extinguishing of their 'I'. Meister Eckhart found an excellent word to describe this descending into his own inner self. He spoke of 'un-becoming', that is to say the extinction of the 'I'. And we read in the *Theologia Germanica* how the author describes the mystic path into the inner human being, and how he insists that he who wishes to descend will act no longer through his own 'I', but that Christ, with Whom he is fully permeated, will act within him.[3] Such mystics sought to extinguish their 'I'. Not *they* themselves but *Christ within them* should think, feel and will, so that there may not emerge what dwells within them in the form of passion, desire and greed, but rather that which streams into them as Christ. That is why St. Paul says: 'Not I, but Christ in me.'[4]

We can describe the processes of waking up and falling asleep as inner experiences of the human being: awakening as a sinking down of the compressed 'I' into the corporeality of man, and falling asleep as a liberation from consciousness, because we are not yet ready to see that world into which we penetrate on falling asleep. In that sense we can conceive of waking and sleeping as we need to conceive of many other phenomena of life: as the interpenetration of the various members of the human being. Looking at a person in the state of being awake we can say: 'In the state of being awake four members are present: the physical body, the etheric body, the astral body and the 'I'; they interpenetrate in a particular way. And in what does this result? In the state of being awake!' For a human being could not be awake if it were not for his capacity to descend into his body in such a way that his attention is deflected by the outside world. The human condition of being awake is dependent on a very specifically co-ordinated co-operation of his four members. And in like manner the condition of being asleep depends on the proper separation of these members. It is not enough to state that the human being consists of physical body, etheric body, astral body and 'I'; really to understand the human being we need to know how the various members are related to one another in a particular state of being, how they interpenetrate. This is essential to our understanding human nature. We tend to regard the way the various members are configured during the state of waking as the normal condition.

Let us now start from this assumption of the waking state as the normal condition. Most of you will remember that the consciousness we have at present as earthly people between birth and death is only one of many possible forms of consciousness. If you study *Occult Science*[5] or the earlier essays in *Cosmic Memory*[6] you will find that today's consciousness is one stage among seven different stages of consciousness, and that our present-day consciousness has evolved from three different stages which preceded it and that it will develop into three further stages of consciousness in the future. During his time on old Moon man had not developed the 'I'. The 'I' only united with the human being in the course of the Earth period. Therefore the present form of consciousness only became available to man during the Earth period. For our present form of consciousness between birth and death the 'I' must co-operate with the other three members in exactly the way it does today and it must be the highest member out of the four principles that constitute the human being. Before the human being was impregnated with the 'I' he consisted merely of physical body, etheric body and astral body. His highest member was the astral body and his consciousness was something like that which we have retained as an ancient inheritance in our dream consciousness. However, you must not imagine our present-day dream consciousness, but one which conveyed realities through the images of dreams. If we study the dream as it is today, we shall find in its manifold images much that is chaotic, because our present dream consciousness is an ancient inheritance. But if we study the consciousness that preceded that of today, we should find that we could not at that time see external objects such as plants, for instance. Thus it was impossible for us to receive an external impression. Anything that approached us evoked an impression analogous to that of a dream, but corresponded to a certain external object or impression.

Thus the 'I'-consciousness was preceded by a consciousness related to the astral body which was the highest member. This astral consciousness was dim and nebulous, and not yet irradiated by the light of the 'I'. When the human being became Earth-man, this astral consciousness was outshone by the 'I'-consciousness. The astral body, however, is still within us, and we might ask how it was that our astral consciousness could be so dimmed and eliminated that the 'I'-consciousness could fully take its place? This became possible because, through our impregnation by the 'I', the earlier connection between the astral body and the etheric body was greatly loosened. The earlier and more intimate connection was, so to speak, loosened up. Thus before the 'I'-consciousness there existed a far more intimate relationship between our astral body and the lower members of our being. The astral body penetrated further into the other members than it does today. In a certain respect the astral body has been wrested from the etheric and physical bodies.

We must be quite clear about this process of the partial exit, this detachment, as it were, of the astral body from the etheric and physical bodies. Then the question will arise whether it might be possible today, with our normal 'I'-consciousness, to establish something similar to this ancient relationship? Could it not happen also today in a human life that the astral body tries to penetrate further into the other members than it ought, to impregnate and penetrate more than is its due?

There is, in fact, a certain normal measure for this penetration of the astral body into the etheric and physical bodies. If this is exceeded in one or the other direction certain disturbances in the whole of the human organism will result from this. For what the human being is today depends upon that exact relationship between the various principles of his being which we find in a normal waking state. As soon as the astral body acts wrongly, as soon as it penetrates deeper into the etheric and physical bodies, there will be disorder. In our past discussions we saw that this really takes place. We then looked at the whole process from another aspect. When does this happen?

It happens when in an earlier life the human being impregnated his astral body with something, allowed something to flow into it that we conceive of as a moral or intellectual transgression for that earlier life. This has been engraved on the astral body. When a person enters life anew, this may in fact cause the astral body to seek a different relationship with the physical and etheric bodies than it would have sought had it not in the preceding life been impregnated with this transgression. Thus are the transgressions committed under the influence of Ahriman and Lucifer transformed into organizing forces which, in a new life, induce the astral body to adopt a different relationship towards the physical and etheric bodies than would be the case had such forces not intervened.

So we see how earlier thoughts, sensations and feelings affect the astral body and induce it to bring about disorders in the human organism. What happens when such disorders are brought about? When the astral body penetrates further into the physical and etheric bodies than it normally should, it brings about something similar to what takes place when we awaken, when our 'I' sinks down into the two lower principles. Awakening consists in the sinking down of the 'I'-principle into the physical and etheric bodies. In what then consists the action of the astral body, when, induced by the effects of earlier experiences, it penetrates the physical and etheric bodies further than it should? That which takes place when our 'I' and our astral body sink down into our physical and etheric bodies when we wake up in the morning and start perceiving things shows the very fact of our awakening. Just as the state of waking is the result of the descent of the 'I'-principle into our physical and etheric bodies, something analogous to that activity of the 'I' must now take place for the astral body. It descends into the etheric body and the physical body. In the case of a person whose astral body has a tendency towards a closer union with the etheric and the physical bodies than should normally take place, we can see the astral body accomplish the phenomenon which we otherwise achieve by the 'I' upon awakening. What is this excessive penetration of the physical and etheric bodies by the astral body? It constitutes the essence of illness. When our astral body does what we otherwise do upon awakening, namely pushes its way into the physical body and the etheric body; when the astral body, which normally should not develop any consciousness within us, strives after a consciousness within our physical and etheric bodies, trying to awaken within us, we become ill. Illness is an abnormal waking condition of our astral body. What is it we do when, in normal health, we live in an ordinary waking condition? We are awake in ordinary life. But to achieve the ordinary state of wakefulness we had to bring our astral body into a different relationship at an earlier stage. We had to put it to sleep. During the day, when our 'I'-consciousness prevails, our astral body needs to sleep; we can be healthy only if our astral body is asleep within us. So we can conceive of the essence of health and illness in the following way: illness is an abnormal awakening of the astral body within man, and health is the normal sleeping state of the astral body.

And what is this consciousness of the astral body? If illness really is the awakening of the astral body, something like a consciousness must be manifested. There is an abnormal awakening, and so we can expect an abnormal consciousness. A consciousness of some kind there must be. When we fall ill something similar must happen to what occurs when we awake in the morning. Our faculties must be diverted to something different. Our ordinary consciousness awakens in the morning. Does any consciousness arise when we become ill?

Yes, there arises a consciousness that we know all too well. And which is this consciousness? A consciousness expresses itself in experiences! The consciousness which then arises is expressed in what we call pain, which we do not have during our waking condition when in ordinary health, because it is then that our astral body is asleep. When our astral body is asleep, it is correctly aligned to our physical and etheric bodies, and that means freedom from pain. Pain tells us that the astral body is pressing into the physical body and the etheric body in an excessive way, and is acquiring consciousness. Such is pain.

We must not apply this statement without limits. When we speak in terms of spiritual science we must put limits to our statements. It has been stated that when our astral body awakens, there arises a consciousness that is steeped in pain. We must not conclude from this that pain and illness invariably go together. Without exception, every penetration into the etheric and physical bodies by the astral body constitutes illness, but the inverse does not hold. That illness may have a different character will be shown by the fact that not every illness is accompanied by pain. Most people take no notice of this because they usually do not strive after health, but are satisfied to be without pain; and when they are without pain they believe themselves to be healthy. This is not always the case; but generally in the absence of pain people will believe themselves to be healthy. We should be under a great delusion if we believed that the experience of pain always coincides with illness. Our liver may be damaged through and through, and if the damage is not such that the abdominal wall is affected, there will be no pain at all. We may carry a process of disease within us which in no way manifests itself through pain. This may be so in many instances. Objectively regarded these illnesses are the more serious, for if we experience pain we set to work to rid ourselves of it, but when we have no pain we do not greatly trouble to get rid of the disease.

What is the position in cases where illness is not accompanied by pain? We need but remember that only little by little did we develop into human beings such as we are today, and that it was during this Earth period that we added the 'I' to the astral body, etheric body, and physical body. Further back we only possessed etheric body and physical body. A being possessing only these two principles is like a plant of the present day. We meet here a third degree of consciousness infinitely more vague, which does not attain to the clarity even of today's dream consciousness. It is quite erroneous to believe that we are devoid of consciousness when we sleep. We have a consciousness, but it is so vague that we cannot call it up within our 'I' to the point of memory. Such a consciousness dwells also within plants; it is a kind of sleep consciousness of a still lower degree than the astral consciousness. We have now reached an even lower degree of human consciousness.

Let us suppose that through experiences in previous incarnations we have brought about not only the kind of disorder in our organization which causes the astral body to excessively penetrate the physical and etheric bodies, but have also done something or other which is liable to push the etheric body into the physical body to an inappropriate degree. It is certainly possible for the relationship between the etheric body and the physical body to become abnormal, for the etheric body to penetrate more deeply into the physical body than is appropriate today. Let us suppose that the astral body is not involved at all; but that the tendency created in an earlier life effects a closer connection than there should be between the etheric body and the physical body in the human organism. In that case the etheric body acts in the same way as the astral body does when we have pain.

If the etheric body in its turn penetrates too deeply into the physical body, a consciousness similar to our sleep consciousness arises, something of the nature of plant consciousness. It is not surprising, therefore, that this is a condition of which we are not aware. Anyone unaware of sleep will equally be unaware of this condition. And yet it is a sort of awakening! As our astral body will awake abnormally when it has sunk too deeply into the etheric and physical bodies, so will our etheric body awake in an abnormal manner when it penetrates too deeply into the physical body. But this will not be perceived by us, because it is an awakening to a consciousness even more vague than the consciousness of pain. Let us suppose that a person has really in an earlier life done something that between death and a new birth is so transformed that the etheric body itself awakens, that is, it takes intense possession of the physical body. If that happens there awakes within us a deep consciousness that cannot however be perceived in the same manner as other experiences of the human soul. Must it, however, be ineffectual because it is imperceptible? Let us try to explain the peculiar tendency acquired by a consciousness which lies still one degree deeper.

If you burn yourself – which is an external experience – this causes pain. If a pain is to appear, the consciousness must have at least the degree of consciousness of the astral body. A pain must be in the astral body; thus, whenever pain arises in the human soul, we are dealing with an occurrence in the astral body. Now let us suppose something happens which is not connected with pain, but is, however, an external stimulus, an external impression. If something flies into your eye, this causes an external stimulus and the eye closes. Pain is not connected with it. What does the irritant produce? A movement. This is something similar to what occurs when the sole of your foot is touched; it is not pain, but still the foot twitches. Thus there are also impressions upon a human being which are not accompanied by pain, but which still give rise to some sort of an event, namely, a movement. In this case, because he cannot penetrate down into this deep degree of consciousness, the person does not know how it comes about that a movement follows the external stimulus. When you perceive pain and you thereby repulse something, it is the pain which makes you notice that which you then reject. But now something may come which urges you to an inner movement, to a reflex movement. In this case the consciousness does not descend to the degree at which the irritant is transformed into movement. Here you have a degree of consciousness which does not come into your astral experience, which is not experienced consciously, which runs its course in a kind of sleep consciousness, but may nevertheless result in certain events.

When this deeper penetration of the etheric body into the physical body comes about, it produces a consciousness which is not a pain consciousness, because the astral body takes no part in it, but is so vague that the person does not perceive it. This does not necessarily mean that a person in this state of consciousness is not able to act in a way appropriate to the situation. After all, people act in all sorts of ways that do not involve their consciousness. Just think of cases where the ordinary day consciousness is extinguished and all sorts of acts are performed, such as during sleepwalking. In a case like this there is no absence of consciousness but rather a kind of consciousness which the person cannot share in, because he can only experience the two higher forms of consciousness: the astral consciousness as pleasure and pain and so on, and the 'I'-consciousness as judgement and as ordinary day-consciousness. This does not imply that a human being cannot act out of this sleep consciousness.

So we also have a consciousness which is so deep that we cannot reach it any more when our etheric penetrates into our physical body. Let us assume a case where someone affected in this way nevertheless wishes to do something of which he knows nothing in ordinary life and which is connected with the situation in some way; he will then do it without becoming aware of it. Something within him, namely the thing itself, will do it and he himself will know nothing about it. Let us now consider a person who through certain occurrences in an earlier life has attracted certain causes which during the period between death and a new birth result in a deeper penetration of the etheric into the physical body. In consequence the person concerned will do things which will result in deep-seated disease processes. The person will be urged actually to seek out external causes of illness.

It may seem strange that such things do not become clear to the normal 'I'-consciousness. However, no one would do that out of their normal 'I'-consciousness. Nobody would command themselves to seek out sites of infection out of their normal 'I'-consciousness. But if we assume that the dim consciousness referred to considers it necessary for an outer damage to occur and for what we have termed the meaning of illness yesterday to come into play, then this consciousness which penetrates into the physical body will seek for the cause of illness. It is man's own being which seeks for the cause of illness in order to set in motion what we called the process of illness yesterday. So you will understand out of the deeper nature of illness that counter-effects occur even when there is as yet no pain. And when there is pain, and the etheric body penetrates too deeply into the physical body, a seeking of external causes of illness by deeper layers of human consciousness may result. It may sound grotesque but is nevertheless true: just as we search for our inherited characteristics we search for our outer causes of illness when we need them – with a different degree of consciousness. However, what I have just described only applies within the limits stated today.

My main objective today was to show that a human being may be capable – without being able to follow the process with his familiar consciousness – of searching for an illness through producing an abnormal and lower state of consciousness. We learned that illness implies the awakening of stages of consciousness which as human beings we have long overcome. Our transgressions in an earlier life make us bring forth levels of consciousness lower than what is appropriate to our present life. And what we do out of the impulses of such levels of consciousness affects the course of the disease process as well as the process which leads to illness in the first place.

This shows us that in such abnormal states old stages of consciousness arise which human beings overcame a long time ago. If you just look at everyday life a little more closely you will gain a clearer picture of what has been described today. It is a fact that pain makes us descend more deeply into our being. You will be aware of the saying that we only know that we have a particular organ when it has begun to hurt us. It is a popular saying; but there is wisdom in it. Why do we know nothing about it in our ordinary consciousness? Because normally our consciousness is asleep to an extent where it does not penetrate deeply enough into our astral body. Then, when it does penetrate, pain arises and this pain brings the respective organ to our awareness. In that way many popular expressions contain real wisdom since they represent heirlooms from earlier stages of consciousness when man was still able to gaze into the spiritual world and know much of what we have to acquire with great effort today.

Once you understand that human beings are capable of experiencing deeper layers of consciousness you will also find it possible to understand that human beings may not only seek for external causes of illness but also for strokes of destiny which may seem without reason but whose reason works into deeper layers of consciousness. So one might well think that a person would not ordinarily place himself where lightning will strike him. With his ordinary consciousness he will avoid doing so. But there may be active within him a consciousness that lies deeper than his ordinary consciousness and will lead him to the very place where lightning may strike him, from out of a foresight which his ordinary consciousness lacks; a consciousness which wills the lightning to strike him and makes him seek out this accident.

We have now learned that it is possible to seek out accidents or outer causes of illness due to karmic effects. In due course we will deal with the details of such processes, such as the way in which the forces in deeper levels of consciousness work within the human being, or to what extent our ordinary consciousness may avoid such accidents. We can understand that someone who goes to a place where he may succumb to an infection will have been driven there under the influence of a certain level of consciousness; in like manner we must be able to understand how it is that human beings take certain measures to render such infections less and less effective; in other words, that through our ordinary consciousness we are able to avert certain consequences by means of hygiene. We can grasp the possibility of counteracting certain effects by means of our ordinary consciousness, and we must concede that it would be most unreasonable if our subconscious was capable of seeking out disease-bringing germs if causes of illness could not be avoided through our ordinary consciousness.

We shall see that it is 'reasonable' to seek out disease-bringing germs, and that it is also 'reasonable' to introduce certain measures of hygiene against infection from out of our ordinary consciousness in order to avoid causes of illness.

LECTURE 7

Karma in Relation to the Forces of Nature, Volcanic Eruptions, Earthquakes and Epidemics

Hamburg, 22 May 1910

You will have noticed in these lectures that we are approaching our goal step by step, and that with each step we are trying to penetrate more deeply into our subject. In the last lecture we spoke of the nature of pain, which may be connected with the course of an illness; we also pointed out how in other cases an illness may run its course – at least in a certain sense – without being accompanied by pain.

We must now consider the nature of pain in somewhat more detail. We must keep before us the fact that pain may become apparent side by side with illness. In our last discussion we already concluded that we may not look upon disease and pain as inseparable. We must be aware that if pain is connected with an illness, there must be something more at stake than mere illness. We have pointed out that the process taking place during the transition from one incarnation to another, whereby events of earlier incarnations are transformed into causes of illness, is influenced on the one hand by the luciferic principle and on the other by the ahrimanic principle.

How do we lay the foundation of illnesses? Why do we acquire a predisposition for illness? What induces us between death and a new birth to prepare forces which will manifest as illness in our next life? We are impelled to this when we see our own weakness in the face of the temptations of Lucifer on the one hand and those of Ahriman on the other. All our greed, egotism, ambition, pride, vanity, all qualities connected with a sort of inflation of our ego, with a desire to be in the limelight, all this is the result of luciferic temptations. In other words, if we fall victim to the forces active within our astral body so that they find expression in our egotistical greeds and passions, we are in that incarnation performing actions to which we are tempted by Lucifer. And during the period between death and a new birth we see the results of such deeds inspired by Lucifer. We then contract the tendency to incarnate in conditions where we shall have to suffer an illness which, if it is overcome, will free us still further from the clutches of these luciferic powers. If the luciferic powers did not exist, we should not fall into those temptations that induce us to develop further in that way.

If there were nothing else in life but the egotistical impulses and passions born of Lucifer, we should never be able to free ourselves from them, not even in successive incarnations, for we should ever again succumb to them. Suppose for instance we had been left to our own devices during Earth evolution, but were still subject to the luciferic influence. We should have the temptations of the luciferic powers in one incarnation and then after death perceive where they had led us. This would bring about an illness, but, if nothing else co-operated, the illness would lead to no great improvement during the life in which it is experienced. It leads to an improvement only because other powers whom Lucifer opposes add something to the whole process. In other words, when we succumb to the luciferic powers, the powers whom Lucifer opposes immediately intervene to try and build up an opposing force by which the luciferic influence can actually be driven out of us. And these powers whom the luciferic powers oppose add the sensation of pain to the process caused by Lucifer's influence. So we have to view pain as something which the benevolent powers give us in order that the pain we suffer may wrest us away from the bad powers and help us not to succumb to them again. If the disease process which results from succumbing to the luciferic powers was not accompanied by pain we would simply conclude: It's not so bad after all to yield to the influence of Lucifer! And there would be nothing within us that could make us apply our forces to escape from the luciferic powers. Pain, which is the astral body's consciousness in a wrong waking state, is also that which can help us not to fall prey again to the luciferic powers in that realm where we have already succumbed. In this way pain serves to educate us in relation to luciferic temptations.

Now please don't object: 'How can we be educated by pain when all we do is feel it, without becoming aware of its beneficial powers?'

It is only our 'I'-consciousness which prevents us from attaining such awareness. In the consciousness I described to you as lying beneath our 'I'-consciousness the following takes place even if we don't realize it in our normal waking consciousness: 'Now I am experiencing pain, and this is brought about by the good powers to counteract my transgressions!' This is a force in our subconscious mind acting truly as karmic fulfilment – as an impulse to fall no more into those deeds, inclinations and greeds that brought about the illness.

Thus we see how karma acts, how we fall prey to the luciferic powers, how these powers effect an illness in the following incarnation, and how beneficent forces add pain to the organic trouble, so that through the pain we may educate the subconscious. We may therefore say that in every case where pain makes itself felt, we are dealing with an illness provoked by the luciferic forces. Pain is a sign that the luciferic power lies at its roots. People who go in for classification will now be longing to distinguish these illnesses that are due to purely luciferic influence from those which can be traced to purely ahrimanic influence. For in all theorizing it is most convenient to classify – to make formulæ – and people delude themselves into believing that they have comprehended much in this way. In reality, however, things do not arrange themselves in such a way that they can be grasped in this convenient manner. In reality they continually intercross and interpenetrate. And it will be easy to understand that during the course of an illness there are phenomena which may be attributed in part to Lucifer's influence – to the activities of our astral body – and others which are traced to the ahrimanic influence. Thus no one must believe that if we feel pain, it is attributable only to luciferic influences. Pain reveals that part of our illness is attributable to luciferic influence. But this will become clearer if we ask where the ahrimanic influence originates.

We should not have fallen prey to ahrimanic influence if we had not first succumbed to that of Lucifer. Through the luciferic influence there came about the relation of the four elements constituting the human being – the physical body, etheric body, astral body and the 'I' – a relation which would not have existed if only the powers whom Lucifer opposes had operated. In that case we should have developed quite differently. Thus the luciferic principle caused disorder in the inner being of man. However, it is entirely a question of our inner being how the world outside affects us. Just as we cannot see the world when we have imperfect eyes, so through luciferic influence we are prevented from seeing the external world as it really is. And because of our incapacity to see the external world as it really is, the ahrimanic influence has been able to insinuate itself into this inaccurate picture. So it is the luciferic influence on us which has made Ahriman's approach possible. Due to the ahrimanic influence we can fall prey not only to egotistical passions, urges, greeds, vanity and pride, and so forth, but now egotism can affect the human organism to such an extent as to develop organs through which we see the external world distorted and inaccurate. Ahriman has insinuated himself into this inaccurate picture, and under his influence we succumb not only to inner temptations but also to error. We fall into untruth in our judgement of the external world and our assertions concerning it. Thus Ahriman acts from outside; but we have made it possible for him to reach us.

In that way the ahrimanic and luciferic influences are never separated. They always react upon one another, and in a certain sense keep a balance. Lucifer manifests outwards from within, Ahriman acts from without, and our picture of the world is formed between the two. If in one incarnation the inner human being gains in strength, if that individual is more exposed to the inner influences, then he will succumb more easily to Lucifer, when his pride, his vanity and so on, will come into play. In an incarnation in which a person is not through his general karma predisposed to yield to inner influences, he will be more inclined to fall prey to error and the temptations of Ahriman. This is what actually happens. So that in daily life we at one moment fall prey more to the temptations of Lucifer, and at another to those of Ahriman. And we oscillate between these two influences which lead us – the one to inner conceit, and the other to illusions about the external world.

Since it is a matter of singular importance, I might mention that the temptations from both sides must be especially resisted by anyone who is called to a spiritual development, and who wishes to penetrate into the spiritual world, whether by penetrating into that external spirituality which lies behind the phenomena of the external world, or whether by descending mystically into his own inner being. When we penetrate the world which lies behind the physical world, we always find those deceptive images which Ahriman conjures up. When a person tries to descend mystically into his own soul, he is exposed to the temptations of Lucifer in a special degree. When he tries to descend blissfully without having previously taken precautions against pride, vanity and so forth; when he succeeds in living as a mystic without having given heed to a special moral culture, he is the more liable to fall victim to the temptations of Lucifer, who acts upon the soul from within. If a mystic has not given careful heed to his moral culture, he will be in great danger, when penetrating his inner being, of calling forth even more strongly than before the reactionary forces of Lucifer, and of becoming even more vain and proud than he formerly was. For this reason it is essential first to ensure that through the forming of our character we are able to resist the temptations of vanity, conceit and pride to which we shall be exposed in any case. We can never do enough towards the acquisition of such qualities as lead to modesty and humility. This is essential for that aspect of our development which we call mystic. On the other hand it is necessary to defend ourselves against the delusions of Ahriman when we attempt to reach the spiritual origin of things by following the path which leads behind the phenomena of the external world. If we do not form a strong and steadfast character which enables us to fortify ourselves, to acquire a strong inner life, it may well happen that, just at the moment when we are succeeding in going out into the spiritual world, we fall into the clutches of Ahriman, who will beguile us by illusion upon illusion, hallucination upon hallucination.

I have often found that people take what I say a bit too literally. Because I often emphasize how important it is that any form of spiritual development aimed at penetrating the sense-perceptible world must be undertaken in full consciousness, it happens again and again that people bring along some somnambulist individuals who assure me that they really do perceive the spiritual world, and in full consciousness. The only thing that can be done is to assure them that it would be far better for them, and far wiser, if they did not have this full consciousness. For people are mistaken as to the nature of this 'consciousness', which is merely an image or astral consciousness. If these people were not conscious in a lower degree they would not perceive anything, and what matters is that we should, on entering the spiritual world, maintain the integrity of our 'I'-consciousness. With the 'I'-consciousness, however, is linked our power of judgement and our faculty for acute discrimination. This is what is lacking regarding the forms which they see in the spiritual world. That such people should have some consciousness is in no way remarkable, but the consciousness they should have is that which is linked to the culture of our 'I'. That is why during our development towards the perception of the higher worlds we are not so keen on reaching these higher worlds as speedily as possible, on seeing a world filled with images and all kinds of forms, on hearing perhaps all kinds of voices. Rather do we emphasize the fact that entrance to the spiritual world can only bring happiness or be of advantage when our consciousness, our faculty of discrimination and discernment, and our power of judgement have been so sharpened that in the higher worlds we shall be subject to no delusion. This can best be achieved by studying the truths of spiritual science. For this reason we insist that the study of spiritual science is the best safeguard against these alleged visions, which by their nature are not capable of being brought to the test of a sound judgement. Anyone who is properly schooled in this way will not accept everything that comes his way, but will be able to distinguish between reality and a mirage. He will also know that auditory perceptions must be treated with the greatest circumspection, for no such perceptions can correspond to reality unless the hearer has previously passed through the sphere of absolute silence. Anyone who has not first experienced the absolute silence and calm of the spiritual world may be certain that what he perceives are delusions, even though what they convey to him seems most portentous. Only people who have taken the pains to fortify their judgement through their very efforts at understanding the higher worlds will be protected from such delusions. The means offered by science are insufficient. Science does not provide us with a power of judgement sure enough and strong enough for true discernment in the spiritual world. That is why we say that if information concerning the higher worlds is given us by people who have not carefully fortified their power of judgement – and this can be done through the study of spiritual science – such information is always questionable, and must in any case first be checked by the methods attained through genuine training. From this we see that Lucifer and Ahriman do not suspend their temptations when we strive for a higher development.

There is but one power before which Lucifer retreats, and that is morality, which burns him like the most dreadful of fires. And there is no means by which to oppose Ahriman other than a power of judgement and discernment schooled by spiritual science. For Ahriman flees in terror from the wholesome power of judgement acquired upon earth. In the main there is nothing to which he has a greater aversion than the qualities we gain from a healthy education of our 'I'-consciousness. For we shall see that Ahriman belongs to a very different region far removed from that force of sound judgement which we develop in ourselves. The moment Ahriman encounters this, he receives a terrible shock, for this is something completely unknown to him, and he fears it. The more we apply ourselves in our life to develop this wholesome judgement, the more do we work in opposition to Ahriman. This appears particularly in all kinds of people brought before one, who recount from dawn to sunset all they have seen in the spiritual worlds. And if one attempts to give to these people some explanation, and to develop their judgement and discernment, Ahriman generally has them so completely in his power that they can hardly enter into the discussion. It is even more difficult to get them to listen to reason when Ahriman's temptations come to them from the auditory side. There are many more ways of dealing with delusions which appear as images than with those which come acoustically – in voices heard and so forth. Such people have a great aversion to any serious study that would contribute to the development of their 'I'-consciousness between birth and death. But it is not they themselves who do not like it; it is the ahrimanic forces that drag them away from it. If one leads those people so far as to develop a sound power of judgement, and they begin to accept instruction, it soon becomes evident that the visions, voices and hallucinations cease. They were merely ahrimanic chimera, and Ahriman is possessed by fear as soon as he feels that from out of this person there comes forth a wholesome power of judgement.

In fact, the best remedy against the particularly harmful diseases which result in visions and delusory voices induced by Ahriman is to do everything possible to induce the person to acquire a wholesome and rational judgement. In many such cases this proves extraordinarily difficult, for the other powers make things very easy for the deluded ones and guide them on. But anyone who attempts to expel this power cannot take things as lightly as that, and in consequence finds his task a difficult one; for the people affected in this way will then often maintain that they are being deprived of that which before had led them into the spiritual world. The truth of the matter is that they are being healed and safeguarded against further encroachment by these powers!

We now know what the luciferic and ahrimanic forces abhor. Lucifer is not at all pleased if human beings conduct themselves with humility and modesty, guided by a sound judgement of who they are. On the other hand, he is present, like the flies in the dirty room, whenever the qualities of vanity and ambition arise. All this, and the illusions which we engender about ourselves, prepare us to receive Ahriman as well. Nothing can defend us against Ahriman unless we really make an effort to think wholesomely, as life between birth and death teaches us to do. And especially we, who stand on the rock of spiritual science, have every reason to emphasize again and again, and as strongly as possible, the fact that it is not appropriate for us as earth-beings to disregard that which is to be given us through life upon earth. People who disdain the acquisition of a wholesome judgement and power of discrimination and who aspire to a spiritual world without making this effort are really trying to shun earth life. They, being of the opinion that it is really far too trivial an occupation for them to concern themselves with matters that may lead to an understanding of this life, aspire to soar above it. They consider themselves superior and it is just this frame of mind which constitutes a fresh cause of pride. For this reason we frequently find that people with an inclination to getting carried away, to avoiding contact with the earthly world and all it entails, refuse to learn 'because they are already in the midst of it all' and do not wish to be associated with a movement such as ours. Such people say: Humanity must enter the spiritual world.

Certainly – but there is only *one* healthy path by which we can enter, and that is the morality acquired on earth in a higher sense, a morality that will keep us from over-estimating ourselves, and will make us less subservient to our impulses, greeds and passions; and it is furthermore our active, wholesome interaction with the conditions of earthly life as opposed to wishing to soar above earthly matters.

Here we have drawn from out of the depths of karma something connected with the depths of spiritual life. This may be of great value, but nothing from the spiritual world is of value to the development of the human being and of his individuality unless it be brought forth from the spiritual world with sound reason, and with morality.

When considering all the discussions of our last lecture and those of today we might ask: 'Why should not the luciferic influence, for the very reason that it worked earlier and has been transformed into illness, and then equalized through the pain, why should it not call forth in us, draw after it, as it were, the ahrimanic influence? And why should not that which causes us pain and announces the luciferic influence of a disease, why should not the ahrimanic influence take part in this as a consequence of the luciferic influence? How does the ahrimanic influence work? How are the temptations of Ahriman turned into causes of illness? How do they manifest in later incarnations?'

Whatever is attributable to ahrimanic influence is indirectly attributable to Lucifer; when, however, the luciferic influence has been so strong as immediately to call forth the ahrimanic influence, then this influence is all the more insidious. It anchors itself not only in the transgressions of the astral body, but also in those of the etheric body. It manifests in a consciousness lying deeper than our pain consciousness, causing damage not necessarily accompanied by pain, damage that renders useless the organ which it attacks.

Let us suppose that in one incarnation an ahrimanic influence had been exercised on a person bringing with it certain consequences. Now the individual concerned passes through the period between death and a new birth, and reappears in a new incarnation. Then it will become manifest that some organ has been attacked by Ahriman; in other words, the etheric body has entered this organ more deeply than it should – more deeply than normal. In such a case, precisely because of this defective organ, the person is even more open to the temptations of error which are the work of Ahriman upon earth. By means of the organ which owes its defect to the ahrimanic influence, and into which the etheric body has too deeply penetrated, the person would, if he were to experience the whole of this process, become even more enmeshed in what Ahriman can effect, namely, *maya*. Since nothing produced by the material world as *maya* can be carried into the spiritual world, the spiritual world withdraws further from him. For in that world there is only truth and no illusion. The more we become entangled in the illusions effected by Ahriman, the more are we impelled to enter even further into the external world of the senses, into the illusions of the physical senses, much further than would be the case without the defective organ.

A counteracting effect comes into play, however, just as we have the effect of pain counteracting the luciferic influence. This means that at the very moment when there is a risk of our being linked too closely with the physical world of the senses, and of our losing the forces which could lead us up into the spiritual world, the organ is destroyed; it will either be paralysed or else rendered too weak to be effective. A process of destruction takes place. Thus if we see an organ approaching destruction, we must realize that we owe this to beneficial forces; the organ is taken from us so that we may find our way back into the spiritual world. When there is no other way certain forces do in fact destroy our organs or weaken them so that we may not become too greatly entangled in illusion.

Let us take the case of a person who has a disease of the liver, but such as is not accompanied by pain. We are here dealing with the effect of a preceding ahrimanic influence which has resulted in this disorder in the liver. If this organ had not been taken from him, the forces connected with a deeper penetration by the etheric body would have led him too far into *maya*.

Sagas and myths have always known of the deepest wisdom, and have expressed it. Of this the liver is a very good example. It is an organ most eminently suited to drive us into the physical illusory world, and at the same time the liver is the organ which binds us to the earth. This truth is connected with the fact that precisely that being who, according to the legend, gave us the force to guide us into earthly life and work effectively on earth – namely, Prometheus – should have his liver gnawed by a vulture. A vulture gnaws at his liver, not because this would cause Prometheus any severe pain, for in that case the legend would not correspond with the actual facts. However, legends and myths invariably correspond with physiological facts! The vulture gnaws at the liver because it does not hurt. Because the point was to show that Prometheus was bringing something to humanity through which human beings could become more deeply enmeshed in ahrimanic illusion if it were not for the possibility of compensation. Occult records are always in accord with the truths which we make known in spiritual science.

I have shown you today by a simple analysis of facts that it is the beneficial powers which bring pain to us to react against the influence of Lucifer. Let us compare this with the records of the Old Testament.[1] After Lucifer's influence had made itself felt, as is symbolized by the serpent's temptation of Eve, Lucifer's adversaries had to inflict pain to hinder what Lucifer was trying to achieve in human beings. The power whom Lucifer opposes had to appear and disclose that thenceforth humanity should know pain. This was done by Jehovah, or Yahveh, when He said: 'In sorrow thou shalt bring forth children'.

Without the explanations of spiritual science such accounts in the occult records are usually not interpreted correctly. Later one realizes how profound these records are. That is why you cannot expect me simply to explain things out of a vacuum – without certain conditions being fulfilled. For me to be able to talk at all about the passage: 'In sorrow thou shalt bring forth children,' I had to consider the karmic situation; then the explanation can be given in the right place. Therefore it is not much good to wish for one thing or another to be explained from occult records before the appropriate point in occult development has been reached. It is always regrettable when people ask: 'What does this mean? What is the meaning of that?' We must be patient and wait until we have reached the required stage. For with explanations alone we shall achieve nothing.

Thus we see our life affected by the luciferic powers on the one side, and on the other by the powers whom Lucifer opposes. Furthermore the ahrimanic powers work into our lives, and we must realize that those powers which incapacitate our organs when we fall prey to ahrimanic influences are among the beneficent powers, whose adversary is Ahriman.

What has been said so far will provide you with a good basis for looking deeply into the complicated workings of human nature, and you will conclude as follows: The luciferic powers are those that have remained behind during the ancient Moon period, and today during our Earth evolution they influence human life by means of forces which are really Moon forces. According to the cosmic plan of those powers, for example, whom Lucifer opposes, these Moon forces are not part of our Earth evolution. In this way Lucifer works into the intention of another being.

We can now go back to an earlier epoch. If we accept that on the Moon certain beings remained behind in their development to intervene in human life upon Earth, we may be able to understand that also upon the ancient Sun there remained behind beings who played a part upon the Moon analogous to that played by the luciferic powers upon Earth at present. In the present human being we observe what may be described as a conflict: the conflict between the luciferic powers which penetrate into our astral body, and those powers which affect us only through our earthly achievement. For the powers whom Lucifer opposes can only act upon us through our 'I'. If we acquire a clear insight into, and a true valuation of, ourselves, we do so only with the help of those powers which affect our 'I'. For this we must make use of our 'I'. Therefore we may say that while our 'I' struggles with the luciferic powers, Yahveh, or Jehovah, is fighting within us against Lucifer. That which watches over the ordered cosmic design is fighting against that which rebels against this design and against its exclusiveness. Our innermost being stands in the midst of this strife, between Lucifer and other beings. We ourselves are the battlefield of this struggle, and the fact that we are the battlefield in this fight draws us into karma, but only indirectly, through the fact that this battle is fought against Lucifer. If on the contrary we turn our gaze outward, we are attracted by the influence of the ahrimanic powers. Something is enacted that comes from outside, and here Ahriman enters within us.

We know that the ancient Moon was inhabited by beings who passed through their human stage at that time, as we are now passing through it in the course of Earth evolution. In *Cosmic Memory* and *Occult Science* these beings are referred to as Angels, Angeloi and Dhyanis – the name does not matter.[2] Within these beings a battle similar to the luciferic battle within our own souls took place – a battle provoked by those beings who had remained behind upon the Sun. This battle upon the Moon is in no way concerned with our inner 'I' for on the Moon we did not yet possess our 'I'. It is not concerned with anything in which our 'I' takes part. Upon the Moon it took place 'within the bosom of the Angels'. So these beings developed in a way which was possible only through the influence of the other beings who had stayed behind during the Sun evolution. These beings who played the same part with regard to the Angeloi as the luciferic beings play with regard to ourselves today were the ahrimanic beings which, during the whole of the Sun evolution, remained behind as the luciferic beings did during the Moon evolution. That is why we can only indirectly encounter these beings. It was Ahriman who, as it were, acted as tempter within the breast of the Angeloi, and he was active within them. Because of him the Angeloi had become what they then became, and they have carried over with them what they acquired through Ahriman, as well as what they acquired in positive terms.

One of our positive gains from Lucifer is our ability to

distinguish between good and evil, the free faculty of discrimination, and our free will. All this we may attain only through Lucifer. The Angels, however, have carried over into the Earth the fruits of their struggle with the ahrimanic powers, and this has fitted them for their present task as spiritual beings which surround us. Our inner 'I' is not concerned with and takes no part in what these beings then experienced, nor in the effects of their experiences. We shall see, however, that we receive such experiences indirectly because the ahrimanic influence acts upon us. Through Ahriman, therefore, these beings have attained certain results caused during their Moon existence and these results are introduced into our Earth existence. Let us try to trace in our Earth existence the effect of the ahrimanic battle of that time.

If that ahrimanic battle had not taken place on the ancient Moon, these beings could not bring into our Earth existence that which once formed part of the ancient Moon existence. For that would have ceased to exist after the ancient Moon had perished. Through the ahrimanic influence the Angels became entangled in the Moon existence, just as we, through the luciferic influence, become entangled in Earth existence. They received in their innermost nature something of the Moon element and transported it into our Earth existence. Because of this they are in a position to raise up the forces which will prevent our Earth from succumbing entirely to the luciferic influence. The *whole* of our Earth would have to succumb to Lucifer's influence if the results of the Angels' battle against Ahriman upon the Moon had not been brought into our Earth existence.

What then are the proceedings in the existence of the Earth which we describe as normal? When our present solar system organized itself in accordance with the goal of our Earth, that which we see as the regular movements of the Earth and of the planets began, and brought it about that we have night and day, that the seasons of the year succeed each other in regular succession, that we have sunshine and rain, that our fruits ripen in the fields, and so on. Those are conditions which repeat themselves over and over again according to the rhythm of the cosmos which shaped itself for the present existence after the Moon existence descended into the twilight. But within the Earth existence Lucifer works and we shall see that he works a good deal more than merely in the domain outlined so far, in the human being, which he nevertheless has made his most important domain. Even if Lucifer was only active on earth, human beings would succumb to what we call 'luciferic temptation', not least through the conditions created by the regular course of the planets round the sun, the alternation of summer and winter, rain and sun and so forth. If we were subject to everything that emanates from the order of the cosmos, everything generated by the regular rhythmical movements of the solar system, if only those laws appropriate to our present-day cosmos prevailed, we would be bound to succumb to Lucifer's influence, bound to develop a preference for the easy life over that which we are supposed to attain for our cosmic salvation; we would be bound to prefer the straight and regular course to a path of personal striving.

That is why counter-forces had to be created. Forces were created by certain processes intervening in the regular cosmic processes of our earth existence. These were most beneficial and normal for the ancient Moon but today their activity on earth is abnormal and endangers the regular course of earth evolution. These influences correct in a certain way what would come about as excessive inclination to a comfortable life, to ease and luxury, if the mere rhythmical order prevailed; and we see such forces, for instance,

manifesting in violent hailstorms. So when that which otherwise would be produced by the regular forces of the Earth is
destroyed, a correction is brought about which on the whole
works beneficially – even though man cannot see it at first–
because there is a higher reason at work than can be perceived
by man. When the hail drives down into the fields, we can say
that on the old Moon these forces which work in the hail were
the regular ones, just as those are that work beneficially today
in rain and sunshine; but now they rush in in order to correct
that which otherwise would be produced by the luciferic
influence. And when the regular course is re-established,
they rush in again to effect further correction. Everything that
leads to further progressive evolution belongs to the forces of
the Earth itself. When the volcano throws out its lava, forces
are working in it which are retarded forces brought over from
the old Moon in order that they should bring about a correction in earthly life. This also applies to earthquakes and other
phenomena involving the elements. We shall find that much
that comes from outside finds its justification in the general
course of evolution. We shall see later how this is connected
with the human 'I'-consciousness; many of the questions left
open today will be addressed in that context.

But one point on which we must be clear is that these
matters represent only one side of human existence, of earth
existence, and of the cosmic existence in general. If on the
one hand we see in the destruction of an organ the beneficial
activity of spiritual powers, and if we have found today that
the whole course of earth evolution must be rectified by
forces springing from the ancient Moon existence, we must
now ask how it is that we as earthly people on the other hand
must try to rectify the harmful influences of the ancient Moon
forces. We surely feel that as earthly people we have not the
right to wish for volcanic eruptions and earthquakes, nor may

we ourselves destroy organs in order to assist the beneficial effect of the spiritual powers. At the same time we can rightly say that the outbreak of an epidemic produces something we are seeking in order to compensate for something else. And we can assume that we are driven into certain conditions where we may suffer some injury, the overcoming of which will make us more perfect.

What then of hygienic and sanitary measures? Could one not object: 'If epidemics may prove beneficial, is it not wrong to take measures conducive to health and preventive of disease?' Someone might propose that nothing should be done to obviate natural catastrophes, claiming that this conclusion is entirely supported by what I said yesterday and today.

We will find that this is not the case, but again only on certain conditions. For now we shall be ready – in the course of our next discussion – on the one hand to understand how some organ of ours may be damaged through the workings of beneficial powers so as to prevent us from succumbing to *maya*, and on the other hand to become conscious of the effects we produce by obviating such beneficial influences upon ourselves by means of sanitary and hygienic measures. We will see that we have arrived at a point at which human beings arrive very frequently indeed: When an apparent contradiction emerges and we feel impelled by the total force of that contradiction we come close to the point where the ahrimanic powers can influence us greatly. The likelihood of succumbing to deception is never greater than at a time like this, when we have reached a bottleneck such as this. And it is just as well that we have got into this, because now we can say: 'It is the good powers which render one of our organs useless, since this is a counteraction against Ahriman; therefore one would have to be completely irresponsible not to call for what one might term "the beneficial countermeasures against the ahrimanic powers". After all, measures of hygiene and the like would weaken this beneficial counter-effect.'

We are in a bottleneck. And it is just as well that we have been led to this contradiction for once, so that we may reflect upon the fact that such contradictions are not only possible but even a good discipline for our thinking. For when we have experienced how to get out of this contradiction we will have applied some of our own inner forces, and this can give us the strength to resist Ahriman's deceptions.

LECTURE 8

Karma of the Higher Beings

Hamburg, 25 May 1910

To resolve the contradiction placed before us at the end of yesterday's discussion we need to call to mind again the two forces, the two principles, that have been shown to challenge as well as regulate our karma.

We have seen that our karma is only brought into motion through our suffering the luciferic powers' working in our astral body; these powers tempt us to express our feelings, instincts and passions in ways designed to make us in a certain sense less perfect than we would be otherwise. While acting upon us the luciferic forces call forth the ahrimanic forces that do not act from within but work on us from without; we interact with the world around us and the ahrimanic forces work through what meets us from outside. Thus it is Ahriman who is evoked by Lucifer, and we human beings are vitally involved in the conflict of these two principles. When we find ourselves caught in the clutches of either Lucifer or Ahriman, we must endeavour to progress by triumphing over the ill that has been inflicted upon us. This interplay of activity of the luciferic and ahrimanic powers around us can be understood quite clearly if we consider from a somewhat different aspect the case we alluded to in the last lecture – the case where someone succumbs to ahrimanic influence, whereby he experiences all kinds of deceptive images and illusions. He believes that knowledge of one thing or another has been specially imparted to him, or is in one direction or another making an impression upon him, while another person who had preserved a sound power of judgement would easily recognize that the person in question has succumbed to errors and delusions. Last time we spoke of those cases of clairvoyant delusions regarding the spiritual world, clairvoyance in the invidious sense, and we have also seen that there is no other, or at least no more favourable, defence against the delusions of improper clairvoyance than a sound power of judgement acquired during our physical life between birth and death.

What I said in the last lecture is particularly relevant in cases of misguided clairvoyance. In relation to the kinds of clairvoyance that have not been attained through regular training and properly controlled systematic exercises but which manifest as a result of certain older inherited characteristics in the form of visually perceived images or auditory messages, we will always find that the faculty of clairvoyance eventually diminishes or ceases altogether when the individual concerned finds himself able and inclined to take up serious anthroposophical study or even to embark on a path of genuine and appropriate inner schooling. The real sources of knowledge will always be of help in cases of misguided supersensible perception, provided that the individual concerned is open to them.

But you must be careful to distinguish clearly between the different types of delusions. We all know that if through the complexities of karma someone has arrived at a condition in which he develops symptoms of persecution mania, or megalomania, he will develop a whole system of delusive ideas, all of which he can substantiate most logically but which are nevertheless delusive. It may happen, for instance, that he thinks quite correctly and logically in every other department of life, but has the fixed idea that he is being pursued everywhere for some reason or another. He will be able, wherever he may be, to form the cleverest combinations out of the most trivial happenings: 'Here is that clique again whose one and only aim it is to inflict something or other upon me.' And in the cleverest way he will prove to you how well founded is his suspicion. In that way a person may be perfectly capable of logical thinking and yet give expression to certain symptoms of madness. It will be quite impossible to impress such a person by logical reasoning. On the contrary, if we make use of logical reasoning in such a case it may well happen that this will challenge the delusive ideas and the victim will try and find even more conclusive proof of the assertion resulting from his persecution mania. When we speak in the terms of spiritual science we must be absolutely precise. When I emphasized, now and on a previous occasion, that spiritual-scientific knowledge, when acquired through serious study or even systematic training, is an effective means against aberrant powers of clairvoyance, I referred to a totally different set of circumstances. In the present case we are not concerned with trying to help by means of spiritual science. As a rule one would try and apply ordinary common sense, but people like the one described are absolutely unamenable to it. Why should this be so?

In a disease whose symptoms are such as I have described, we are dealing with a karmic cause related to earlier incarnations, earlier errors. What is manifested as an inner error is not and cannot be caused during the present incarnation. It proceeds from an earlier incarnation. Let us now try and get an idea of how something like this can be carried from an earlier into the present incarnation.

For this purpose we must envisage the course of our soul evolution. Outwardly we consist of physical body, etheric body and astral body. In the course of time, we have built into these sheaths, by means of our 'I', the sentient soul into the astral body, the rational or mind soul into the etheric body, and the consciousness soul into the physical body. These three soul members we have developed and have built into the three sheaths where they now dwell. Let us suppose that in some incarnation we were so tempted by Lucifer, or in other words, we developed such egotistical impulses, greed and other instincts, that our soul was laden with transgressions. These transgressions may be in the sentient soul, the rational or mind soul, or in the consciousness soul. This then is the cause which in some future incarnation will be implanted in one of the three soul members. Let us suppose that there was a fault attributable especially to the forces of the rational soul. In the state between death and a new birth this will be so metamorphosed that it will be manifested in the etheric body. Thus in the new incarnation we encounter in the etheric body an effect that may be traced back to a cause in the rational soul of a preceding incarnation. But the rational soul of the next incarnation will again work independently in that incarnation, and it makes a difference whether this human being has previously committed this transgression or not. If he has committed it in an earlier incarnation, he now carries his fault in his etheric body. It is now deeper rooted and is not in the rational soul but in the etheric body. But such rationality and good sense as we may acquire upon the physical plane will affect only our rational soul, and will not affect the activity of our rational soul in an earlier incarnation which has already been woven into the etheric body. For this reason it may happen that the forces of the rational soul, as we now encounter them in human beings, are doing their work logically, so that the real inner being is altogether intact; but that the co-operation of the rational soul with the diseased part of the etheric body provokes error in a certain direction. In such a case it is possible to reach the rational soul by means of the kind of reasoning we employ on the physical plane, but not the etheric body. That is why neither logic nor persuasion will have any effect. Logic would be of little use were we to place someone in front of a convex mirror so that he could see his distorted image, and then try to convince him that he is mistaken in thus seeing the image. He will nevertheless see a distorted image. In the same way the deluded ideas of a person are something quite separate from him, because his otherwise sound logic is not reflected in a sound manner by his etheric body.

Thus we can carry within our deep organism the karmic effects of earlier incarnations, and it is actually possible to show that the defect is present in a certain part of the organism, as in our etheric body for instance. It shows us what we have provoked in an earlier incarnation through the luciferic influence, and transformed subsequently. And the transformation from something inner to something outer takes place in the period between death and a new birth. Then Ahriman works his way towards us from out of our own etheric body. This is how Lucifer draws Ahriman towards our own etheric body. While the earlier transgression was luciferic, the receipt, as it were, is issued by Ahriman in the next incarnation. Then we have to free ourselves of the damage inflicted on our etheric body. This can only be achieved by working into deeper layers of our organism, and that itself requires more than the application of ordinary reason in one incarnation.

A person displaying symptoms of paranoia in a particular incarnation will be confronted with everything he has done as a result of this ahrimanic injury after passing through the portal of death, and he will live through the utter absurdity of the actions concerned. This in turn will foster in him the strength that will profoundly heal him for his next incarnation. For he can only be healed if that which he committed under the influence of the respective symptoms strikes him as absurd in the time to come in the outer world. This shows you how it is possible to support such healing. Logical reasoning is suited least of all to curing someone suffering from delusions; it will only call forth opposition. But you will be able to help by enabling the person – and this applies particularly to cases where such symptoms are manifested in early youth – to experience the nonsensical nature of his actions in all their crassness, by confronting him with facts whose crass nonsense will react back upon him. In this way a certain amount of healing can be achieved.

You can also contribute to healing when the truths of spiritual science have truly become the inner possession of your soul. When they have become the inner possession of your soul to the extent that they become an integral part of you, your faith will be the strongest imaginable; then your entire being will radiate these truths of spiritual science. These truths stream into the life between birth and death, enriching it, and at the same time reaching far beyond this life; with these truths, which represent knowledge of the supersensible world, you will achieve much deeper effects than with the truths of outer reason. While outer logical reasoning will get you nowhere, you will – provided you have enough time and opportunity – be able to apply the truths of spiritual science in your dealings with the person concerned; the impulses given in this way have power to achieve in this incarnation what could otherwise only be achieved during the transition from one to the next incarnation, namely to work into the etheric body from the rational soul. For the truths of the physical plane can in no way bridge the chasm between the sentient soul and the astral body, between the rational soul and the etheric body or even between the consciousness soul and the physical body. That is why we find over and over again that the tremendous wisdom somebody may have acquired on the physical plane about the sense-perceptible world bears very little relation to his world of feeling, to all the impulses and desires that permeate his astral body. Therefore it is quite possible for a person to be ever so well educated, to possess much theoretical knowledge about matters relating to the physical world, to become something of an old professor – and yet fail to transform his drives and feelings and desires which relate to the astral body. He may know a lot about the physical world and yet be a gross egotist because he absorbed the impulses associated with egotism in his youth. Of course the two things can go hand in hand, the acquisition of knowledge about the outer world of the senses and a transformation of the astral and etheric bodies from within. And it is equally possible for a human being to absorb intellectual knowledge, to apply the forces of his rational soul to the physical plane and yet fail to bridge that deep chasm between his rational soul and his etheric body. In other words, you will find again and again that knowledge of the outer world – however immense – rarely has the power to work into the formative forces of the body.

When knowledge and truth really take hold of a person's entire being you will find that this changes his physiognomy in the course of ten years and that you will be able to read in his face how he has struggled, or wrestled with certain questions in his heart, for example.[1] His gestures, too, will tell you that he has attained calmness through inner efforts. These things find their way into the human organism's formative forces, affecting its most subtle structures. Whatever an individual absorbs spiritually thus works into the most subtle parts of his entire organization. When the things which affect our soul relate to more than just the physical plane we change fundamentally in the course of ten years. The change will reflect the way in which we educate and change that which is within us. It is quite possible for one's facial expression to change in the course of ten years, but unless the abyss has been bridged by inner means the change will have been caused by external influences. In such a case the force of change was not an inner transforming power. This shows us that it is only the spiritual, which really unites with our innermost being, that has the power of deeply affecting our formative forces even in the period between our birth and our death, and that this transition, this bridging of the abyss, takes place through the working of karma between death and a new birth. For example, when all that the sentient soul lived through sinks into those worlds we pass through between death and a new birth, it will, without fail, emerge as formative power in the next incarnation.

In this way the reciprocal activity of Ahriman and Lucifer has become intelligible. And now we will see how this combined reciprocal activity presents itself when things are even more distant, when, for instance, the luciferic influence has not only to cross the abyss between the intellectual soul and the etheric body, but has, as it were, a longer way to go.

Let us suppose that in one life we are particularly susceptible to the influence of Lucifer. In such a case, we should with the whole of our inner being become considerably less perfect than we were before, and in the kamaloca period we should have this most vividly before our eyes, so that we should resolve to make a tremendous effort in order to balance this imperfection. This desire we incorporate as tendency, and in the next incarnation, with what have now become formative forces, we shape our new organism so that it must have a tendency towards balancing our earlier experiences. But let us suppose that the release of these luciferic influences had been instigated by something external, by an external desire. Again this must have been owing to the influence of Lucifer. The external could not have affected us had not Lucifer been active within us. Thus we have within us a tendency to compensate for that which we have become through the luciferic influence.

But as we have seen, the luciferic influence of one incarnation challenges and attracts to itself the ahrimanic influence in the next incarnation, so that the two act in alternation. We have seen the luciferic influence to be such that we can perceive it with our consciousness, that is, our consciousness can just about reach down into our astral body. We have said that it is owing to the luciferic influence when we are conscious of pain. However, we cannot reach down into what one might call the consciousness of our etheric body and physical body. It is true, even in dreamless sleep we have a consciousness, but one of so low a degree that we have no knowledge of it in ordinary life. But this does not necessarily mean that we are inactive in this consciousness. Plants, consisting as they do only of physical and etheric bodies, have this consciousness. Plants live continually in the consciousness of dreamless sleep. The consciousness of our etheric and physical bodies is present also in our waking condition in the daytime, but we cannot reach down to it. That this consciousness may be active, however, is shown when we perform in our sleep somnambulistic actions of which we later know nothing. It is this dreamless sleep consciousness that is active. The ordinary 'I'-consciousness and the astral consciousness cannot penetrate to the sphere of somnambulistic action. However, we should not conclude, from the fact that in the daytime we live in our 'I'-consciousness and our astral consciousness, that the other types of consciousness are absent. We are just not aware of them. Let us suppose that we have provoked a strong ahrimanic influence through a luciferic influence in an earlier incarnation; this ahrimanic influence will then not be able to work into our ordinary consciousness. But it will take hold of the consciousness that dwells within our etheric body, and this consciousness will then not only make us organize our etheric body in a particular way but even induce us to perform acts whose effects will make our etheric body's consciousness say: 'Now you may only purge from within you what the luciferic influence to which you succumbed so strongly in the earlier incarnation has caused in you; and this you may achieve by acting in a way opposite to the earlier luciferic transgression!'

Suppose that a luciferic influence had caused us to abandon our earlier religious or spiritual way of life in favour of one where we said: 'I want to enjoy life!' – in other words, we took a mighty leap into the world of the senses. This would challenge the ahrimanic influence in such a way as to provoke the opposite process. It then happens that passing through life we seek a spot where it is possible in one leap to return to spirituality from a life of the senses. In the one we went with one plunge into gross material pleasures, and in the other we try by one leap to return to a spiritual life. Our ordinary consciousness is not aware of this, but the mysterious subconsciousness which is chained to the physical body and the etheric body now urges us towards a place where we may await a thunderstorm, where there is an oak, a bench placed beneath, and where the lightning will strike. In this case the subconscious mind has urged us to make good what we have done in an earlier incarnation. Here we see the opposite process. This is what is meant by an effect of luciferic influence in an earlier life, and, as a consequence, an

ahrimanic influence in the present life. Ahriman's coopera-
tion is necessary to enable us to put aside our ordinary
consciousness to such an extent that our whole being will
obey exclusively the consciousness of the etheric or of the
physical body. In this way many events become comprehensible. However, we must beware of concluding that every
case of sudden death or severe injury, for example, should be
traced to something similar, for this would be taking a very
narrow view of karma. But there are ways of thinking, even
in our anthroposophical movement, that display a really
narrow view of karma. There are people who believe that
their understanding of karma will lead them to a higher point
of view, but who actually know very little about it. Were
karma really as they conceive of it, the whole world order
would have to be specially arranged in the interests of each
single human being; so that each life should run harmoni-
ously and be duly compensated, the conditions of one life
would always be combined in such a way as to result in an
exact balancing of the consequences of an earlier life. But
such a viewpoint is untenable. Suppose someone were to say
to a man who had met with an accident: 'This is your karma;
this is the karmic result of your earlier life, and you at that
time brought it on yourself.' Were the same man to have some
stroke of luck, then the other would say: 'This can be traced
back to a good deed you did in an earlier life.' If such words
are to have any value, the person should have known what
happened in an earlier life which is supposed to have produced this result. If he had knowledge of that earlier life, he
would see the causes coming from that life, and he would then
have to look towards later incarnations for the effects. The
logical conclusion from this is as follows: In every incarnation certain things happen which are *first time events* in the
life of every human being as it evolves from incarnation to

incarnation, and these will be karmically balanced in the next life. When one then examines the effects in the next life it is possible to look back at the causes. If an accident happens, however, for which in spite of all means at our disposal we can find no causes in an earlier life, then we must allow for the fact that this will be balanced in a later life. Karma is not fate. From every life something is carried into later lives.

If we understand this, we shall also understand that we may find new events in our life which are of profound significance. Let us remember that the great events in the course of human evolution could not come about without being carried by certain people. At a certain moment people must take over the intentions of evolution. What would the development of the Middle Ages have been, had not Charlemagne intervened at a given moment![2] How could the spiritual life of olden times have developed if Aristotle had not at a certain time done his work![3] Always remember that you must conceive of Aristotle living in the very period in which he lived, if you want to understand the course of human evolution; because without him many things would have turned out differently later on. We see from this that people like Charlemagne, Aristotle, Luther and so on did not live at a certain period for their own sakes but for the sake of the world. Nevertheless, their personal destinies are intimately connected with world events. Should we conclude from this, however, that what they accomplished is the expiation or the recompense for their previous merits or transgressions?

Take the case of Luther.[4] You cannot just simply ascribe everything he experienced and endured to his karma; you must be clear that those things which are due to happen in the course of human evolution must come about through human agency and that these individual agents have to be brought out of the spiritual world, without consideration whether they are fully ready in themselves. They are born for the purposes of human evolution, and a karmic path has to be interrupted or lengthened, so that the individuality concerned may appear at a certain time. In such cases a destiny is thrust upon specific individuals which need have no relation to their past karma. But to have achieved something between birth and death sets up on earth later karmic causes, so that though it is true that a Luther was born for humanity and had to bear a destiny which had no connection with his former karma, yet what he accomplished on earth will be connected with his later karma. Karma is a universal law, and everyone is subject to it. But we must not only look back to our former incarnations; we must also look forward. From this point of view it is only in a subsequent life that we can judge and justify earlier incarnations, for some of the events of this life do not lie in the karmic path.

Let us take a case which actually happened. In a natural catastrophe a number of people perished. It is not at all necessary to believe that it was in their karma that they all should thus perish together; this would be a cheap supposition. It should not be assumed that everything is attributable to earlier transgressions. There is an instance, that has been investigated, of a number of people who perished in an elemental catastrophe. This in turn caused these people to feel very closely connected at a later time and, owing to their common destiny, they gained the strength to accomplish something important together. Through this catastrophe they were able to turn from materialism and brought with them in their next incarnation a disposition to spirituality.

What happened in that case? If we go back to the previous life we find that in this instance their shared destruction took place during an earthquake; at the moment of the earthquake the futility of materialism presented itself to their souls, and so a mind directed towards the spiritual developed within them.[5] We can see from this how people whose mission it was to bring something spiritual into the world were prepared for it in this way, which demonstrates the wisdom of evolution. This case has been investigated and authenticated by spiritual science. So we can show how primary events can enter human life, and that it cannot always be traced back to an earlier transgression if one person or several people meet with an early death in a catastrophe or an accident. Such an event may appear as a primary cause, and will be balanced in the next life.

There may be other variations. It may happen that someone has to meet with an early death in two or three consecutive incarnations. This can happen because the individuality in question has been chosen to bring to mankind in the course of three incarnations certain gifts that can be given only when living in the material world with such forces as result from a 'growing' body. To be living in a body that has developed up to the thirty-fifth year is quite different from living in a body of greater age. For up to our thirty-fifth year we direct our forces towards the body, so that the forces unfold from within. But then, starting with the thirty-fifth year, we only progress inwardly, and our life-forces are continually engaged in battling against the forces from outside. From the point of view of the inner organization, these two halves of life differ in every respect from one another. Let us suppose that according to the wisdom which presides over human evolution we stand in need of such people who can flourish only when they do not have to fight against what comes towards us in the second half of life. It may then be that their incarnations are brought to a premature close. There are such cases. At our meetings we have already pointed to an individuality who appeared successively as a great prophet, a great painter, and a great poet and whose life was always brought to an end through premature death, because what had to be accomplished by this individuality in the course of these three incarnations could only be achieved if these incarnations were terminated before he entered the second half of life.[6] Here we see the strange interlacing of individual human karma and the general karma of mankind.

We can go still further and find certain karmic causes in the general karma of humanity whose effects show only at a later period. Thus the individual again sees himself caught up into the general karma of humanity. If we consider the post-Atlantean evolution, we find the Græco-Latin period in the middle, preceded by the Egyptian-Chaldean period and, followed by our period – the fifth cultural epoch. Our period will be followed by a sixth and seventh cultural epoch. I have also pointed out on other occasions that in a certain respect there are cycles in succession of the various civilizations, so that the Græco-Latin culture stands by itself, but that the Egyptian-Chaldean period is repeated in our own. In the present cycle of lectures, I have already pointed out that Kepler lived in our period, and that the same individuality lived earlier in an Egyptian body, and was in that incarnation under the influence of the wise Egyptian priests who directed his gaze to the celestial vault, so that the mysteries of the stars were revealed to him from above.[7] All this was brought further in his Kepler-incarnation which took place in the fifth period, and which, in a certain way, is a repetition of the third.

But we can go still further. From the spiritual-scientific point of view one can honestly say that most people are still fairly blind when it comes to the evolution of the world and human life. These correspondences, these repetitions, these cyclic lives could be followed in great detail. If we take a certain moment in human evolution, say for instance the year

747 B.C., we shall find that it constitutes a sort of hypomochlion, a kind of zero point, and that what lies before and after this point corresponds in quite a definite way. We can go back to an epoch of the Egyptian evolution, and there we find certain ceremonial laws and commandments which appeared as given by the gods. And this they actually were. There were commandments which related to certain ablutions which the Egyptians had to perform by day. They were regulated by custom and by certain ritualistic prescriptions, and the Egyptians were told that they could only live in the manner desired by the gods if on this or that day they were to undertake a certain number of ablutions. This was a commandment of the gods that found expression in a certain cult of cleanliness, and if in the interim we encounter a period somewhat less clean, we now again, in our own period, encounter hygienic measures such as are given to humanity for materialistic reasons. Here we see a repetition of what was lost at a corresponding period in Egypt. The fulfilment of what happened earlier is represented in the general karma in a most remarkable manner. Only the general character is always different. Kepler in his Egyptian incarnation had directed his gaze up to the starry sky, and what that individuality perceived there was expressed in the great spiritual truths of Egyptian astrology. In his reincarnation during the age of materialism the same individuality expressed these facts in a manner corresponding with our period, in his three materialistically coloured 'Kepler's laws'. In ancient Egypt the laws of cleanliness were laws of 'Divine revelation'. The Egyptian believed that he could only fulfil his duty to humanity by going to incredible lengths to ensure his personal cleanliness at all times. This preoccupation with cleanliness comes to the fore again today, but under the influence of a mentality which is entirely materialistic. Modern man does not think that he is

serving the gods when he is obeying such rules, but that he is serving himself. It is nevertheless a reappearance of what went before. This is how everything in the world is fulfilled, totally cyclically, in a certain sense. And now you will begin to understand that the matters we summarized last time in a contradiction are not as simple as one might think. If at a certain period people were not able to take certain measures against epidemics, then these were times when people could not do so because, according to the general wise world plan, the epidemics had to take effect in order to give human souls an opportunity of balancing what had been effected through the ahrimanic influence and certain earlier luciferic influences. If other conditions are now being brought about, this is again due to certain great karmic laws. This shows us that we really must not consider such matters superficially.

How does this agree with our statement that if someone seeks an opportunity of being infected in an epidemic, this is the result of the necessary reaction against an earlier karmic cause. Have we the right now to take hygienic or other measures?

This is a profound question, and we should consider it from all appropriate angles. We must understand that where the luciferic and ahrimanic principles are co-operating or coun-teracting each other – whether concurrently or over longer periods – certain complications in human life will ensue. These complications appear in forms so diverse that we never see two identical cases. If we study human life, however, we shall find our way in the following manner: if in a particular case we try to discover the combined activity of Lucifer and Ahriman, we shall always find a thread by which this connec-tion will become clear. We must discriminate clearly between internal and external man. We were already called upon today to differentiate sharply between that which is expressed by the rational soul, and that which appears within the etheric body as an effect of the rational soul. We need to look at the train of events in which karma is fulfilled, always keeping in mind that there is the possibility at all times for appropriate karmic influences to affect our inner being in such a way that through this inner being different karmic compensations are prepared for future times. For this reason the following may well happen:

In an earlier life we might have lived through intense feelings that drove us to act in an unloving manner towards our nearest and dearest. Let us imagine, for example, that we experienced something which karmically produced an un-loving nature. It is certainly possible that we generate something bad as if on a downward spiral, in other words, that we descend to a certain point in order to develop the opposite impetus which will help us rise up again. So let us assume that due to our yielding to a particular influence we have devel-oped a tendency towards a certain unloving nature; this unloving nature will then manifest in a later life as a karmic effect and will produce inner forces in our organism. Now we may act in two ways, consciously or unconsciously. Our culture has not yet reached the stage to do it consciously. We can ensure that those characteristics that stem from an unlov-ing nature are driven out of the organism of the person affected. We can introduce an antidote against the effect in the outer organism which manifests as an unloving nature; however, such action would only do away with the outer organ of lovelessness, and not cure all the unloving substance in the soul. If we do nothing else we have left the job half-done, and have possibly achieved nothing at all. We may have helped the person physically, externally; but we will have done nothing for his soul. Now that we have deprived him of the outer organ for expressing his unloving nature he can express it no longer; he has to retain it in his inner organism for a future incarnation.

Suppose that a great number of people had felt impelled – due to their unloving attitude to their fellow human beings – to absorb certain infectious substances in order to succumb to an epidemic. Let us further suppose that we could do something about this epidemic. In that case we would prevent the outer physical nature from expressing the unloving disposition while failing to remove the inner inclination to unlovingness. What we need to envisage now is the following: By removing the outer organ of unlovingness we actually incur an obligation of working into the soul in such a way as to remove its inclination to unlovingness. The organ of unlovingness is killed in the most complete sense – in the outer physical sense – through the smallpox vaccination. Spiritual scientific research has shown, for example, that smallpox developed during a time when the general inclination towards egotism and unlovingness reached a particular climax. That is when smallpox emerged in the outer organism. This is a fact. In anthroposophy it is our duty to speak truthfully.

This will enable you to understand why vaccination was introduced in our time. You will also understand why the best minds of our time display a kind of aversion against the practice of vaccination. This aversion corresponds to something within, it is the outer expression of an inner reality. What I would like to say is this: If on the one hand we kill the organ we incur an obligation to follow suit by working to transform the respective person's materialistic nature by means of a spiritually orientated education. This would be the necessary counterpart of our measure. Without it our work is incomplete. Indeed, we are merely accomplishing something to which the person in question will somehow have to produce a counterpart in a later incarnation when he has the smallpox poison within him while the inner characteristic predisposing him to smallpox has been removed. If we destroy the susceptibility to smallpox, we are concentrating only on the external side of karmic activity. If on the one side we go in for hygiene, it is necessary that on the other we should feel it our duty to contribute to the person whose organism has been so transformed something also for the good of his soul. Vaccination will not be harmful if, subsequent to vaccination, the person receives a spiritual education. If we concentrate upon one side only and lay no emphasis upon the other, we weigh down the balance unevenly. This is really what is felt in those circles which maintain that, where hygienic measures go too far, only weak natures will be propagated. This of course is not justifiable, but you will see how essential it is that we should not undertake one task without the other.

Here we approach an important law of human evolution which acts so that the external and the internal must always be counter-balanced, and that it is not appropriate to act with regard to the one only, leaving the other out of consideration. Here we get a glimpse of an important relationship, and yet we have not even arrived at the significance of the question: What is the relationship between hygiene and karma? You will find that the answer to this question will lead us even further into the depths of karma. We shall deal with the karmic connection between birth and death as well as the ways in which other people affect our lives; you will also learn how the human being's free will is in accord with karma.

LECTURE 9

Karmic Effects of our Experiences. Karma in Relation to Death and Birth

Hamburg, 26 May 1910

As I have already pointed out on previous occasions I will only be able to give you an outline of the great laws of karma which might awaken your interest in this almost immeasurable field. If you consider everything we have discussed in the last few days it will not surprise you greatly to hear that the human being is virtually driven – from out of certain layers of his consciousness – to seek, also in the outside world, for the compensating effects of karmic causes acquired earlier. Thus people may virtually be driven to places where it is possible to get an infection in order to find in this the compensating effects for certain karmic causes within them; people are even driven to what one might call fatal life events to find such compensation.

How does it affect the course of karma if measures are taken which result in people being prevented from seeking this kind of compensation?

Let us assume that certain causes, certain circumstances towards which someone might incline as a result of his karma, simply do not exist any more as a result of measures of hygiene having been introduced. Imagine that particular germs had been combated successfully by a programme of hygiene. We have already acquainted ourselves with the idea that it is not at all through human agency that such things come about. We have seen how the tendency to regulate matters of hygiene and sanitation reappears by its reversed repetition in evolution in a certain period, having disappeared in the interim. We learned that it is the great laws of humanity's karma as a whole which determine that such measures are adopted by man at a particular point in time. At the same time we can easily grasp that human beings were not led to adopt such measures at an earlier time because the epidemics which are now to be banished by means of hygienic measures were needed by humanity in an earlier epoch. With regard to major developments in life, human evolution really is subject to definite laws, and we are not in a position to adopt such measures until they will be of significance and value for the whole of human evolution. For these measures do not spring from the fully conscious life, from the rational life between birth and death, but they spring rather from the general mind of humanity. Just call to mind how one invention or discovery or another, too, only occurs when humanity is really ready for it. A brief survey of the history of human evolution upon earth may prove useful.

Let us not forget that our ancestors – that is to say our own souls – dwelt upon the old Atlantean continent in bodies quite different from the present human body. That continent was then submerged and it was only after a definite period that the inhabitants upon the one half of the earth which had emerged were brought into contact with those of the other half. It is only recently that the peoples of Europe have been able again to reach those territories that had emerged on the other side of the submerged Atlantean continent. Indeed, such matters are ordered by great laws. The discovery of one thing or another, the adoption of measures which make it possible to intervene in the realm of karma – these things are not dependent on human beings' opinions or arbitrary decisions, but they arrive when they are due to arrive. Nevertheless, we can influence a person's karma by removing certain causes which would otherwise have existed, and which would have come to him as a karmic fulfilment. This 'influencing' does not mean that we have removed it, but merely that we have changed its direction. Let us suppose that a certain number of people are impelled by karma to seek for certain conditions which would represent to them a karmic compensation. Through hygienic measures these conditions have been removed for the time being and can no longer be met. These people, however, will not be liberated from the karmic effect evoked by their inner being, but will instead be urged to seek other effects. Man cannot escape his karma. Through such measures he is not freed from that which he would otherwise have sought.

From this we may conclude that if the karmic reparation is escaped in one direction, it will have to be sought in another. When we abolish certain influences, we merely create the necessity of seeking other opportunities and influences. Let us assume that many epidemics, communal causes of illness, can be traced to the fact that victims are seeking to remove what they have karmically fostered within themselves. This is the case, for instance, with smallpox which is the organ of unlovingness. Although we may be in a position to remove the possibility of this disease, the cause of unlovingness would still remain, and the souls in question would then be forced to seek another way for karmic compensation either in this or in another incarnation. To help you understand this I will say a few words about something which is very significant in this context.

It is a fact that, at the present time, a whole lot of influences and causes are removed which would otherwise have been sought for as adjustment for certain karmic matters with which mankind had burdened itself in earlier periods. But in removing these influences we only remove the possibility of man's succumbing to their external effects. In this way human life is rendered more comfortable, and also healthier, outwardly. However, all that is achieved is that human beings now have to seek elsewhere for the karmic compensation associated with particular forms of illness. People whose health is spared in this way today are at the same time condemned to seek a karmic adjustment in another way. And they really do have to search for it in numerous cases similar to the one described. When life becomes physically more comfortable due to improved health conditions, the soul is affected in the opposite way; in the course of time the soul experiences a certain emptiness, a sense of dissatisfaction, a lack of fulfilment. If the trend towards ever greater physical comfort and health continued along the lines envisaged in the context of a purely materialistic outlook on life, such souls would feel less and less incentive to progress inwardly. The whole thing would be accompanied by a stultification of the soul.

If you take a closer look at life you will see signs of this already. There has hardly been an age before ours in which so many people live in such pleasant outer conditions and yet go about with their souls barren and unoccupied. That is why such people rush from sensation to sensation; if they have enough money they travel from town to town in order to see something; if not, they rush from pleasure to pleasure every night. Yet for all this the soul remains empty, and ends up at a complete loss about what to look for in the world to fill the void. Especially when life is exclusively geared to outer physical comfort, the inclination to think solely in terms of the physical will be strong. And if this inclination to deal only with the physical world had not already been prevalent for a long time, the inclination towards theoretical materialism would not have arisen to the extent we have it today. In this way human souls are becoming more sick as physical life is rendered more healthy.

Anthroposophists have least call to complain about this, since anthroposophy offers us the possibility to understand these matters and arrive at certain insights as to where compensation may be sought. Souls can only remain empty to a certain degree; then, as if through an inherent elasticity, they are bounced to the opposite. They then seek a content related to their own souls and will then often find how badly they need to attain to a spiritual-scientific view of the world.

This shows us how a materialistic approach to life may well ease things on the physical side but will at the same time create inner difficulties, which may then lead the individual concerned to seek for the content of a spiritual view of life out of his soul's suffering. The spiritual view of life encompassed today in anthroposophy meets those souls who find no satisfaction in the bleakness of impressions offered them by a purely external life, however comfortable it may be. Souls will continue in their search, and seek ever again for new impressions, until their elasticity will act so strongly in the other direction that they will feel themselves again drawn to a spiritual life. Thus there exists a relationship between hygiene and the aspirations for a future spiritual-scientific view of the world.

The beginnings of this are already noticeable today. There are people who add to other superficialities a new superficiality, namely, an interest in the anthroposophical world conception; such people will take up the anthroposophical world conception for the sheer sensation. It is inevitable that what is of profound inner significance also appears as fashion, as sensation, and this tendency can be traced in every current of human evolution. But those souls who are truly ripe for anthroposophy are those who fail to find satisfaction from external sensations, and who realize that natural science, in spite of all its explanations, cannot explain certain facts. These are the souls who through their general karma are so prepared that they become united to anthroposophy with the innermost members of their soul life. Spiritual science forms part of mankind's general karma, and as such will take its place there.

Thus the karma of human beings can be redirected to a certain extent, but its effects on human beings cannot be prevented. What we have prepared for ourselves in earlier lives is bound to be fulfilled in one way or another.

We can show how logical is the working out of karma in the world by considering karma where its activity is still independent of morality – where we see it manifest in the universe, without concerning itself with the moral impulses emanating from the soul of man and leading him to moral or immoral deeds. We shall set before ourselves an aspect of karma in which morality plays no part, but in which something neutral appears as a karmic link.

Let us suppose that a woman lives in a certain incarnation. It cannot be denied that this woman, by reason of her sex, will undergo experiences which differ from those of a man, and that these are not merely dependent on her inner soul life, but are connected predominantly with external happenings, with circumstances in which she will find herself simply because she is a woman, and which will in turn react upon the whole of the state and disposition of her soul. It is reasonable to say that women are led to act in ways which are intimately connected with the fact of being a woman. After all, it is only in the realm of spiritual companionship that the male and the female are balanced. The further we penetrate into the pure soul nature and the outer aspect of the human being, the more accentuated we find the differences between men and women in relation to their lives.[1] We can say that women differ from men also in certain soul qualities, that they have a greater inclination to those qualities of soul which lead to impulses that can only be termed emotional. Women are more disposed to soul experience than men. Intellectuality and materialism – in other words, that which has come about through men – are more natural to men's lives, and this deeply affects their soul life. A closer connection with the soul and the feelings in the case of the woman, and with the intellectual and materialistic in the case of the man – this is how it is actually determined by their respective natures. This is why women display certain nuances in their soul life by virtue of being female.

I have already described to you how that which we experience as qualities in the soul between death and a new birth forces its way into our next bodily organization. That which is related more strongly to the psyche, to the emotions, and tends more towards the inner soul between birth and death will have a greater tendency to enter more profoundly into the organism, and to impregnate it far more intensely. And women, through their aptitude to absorb impressions related to the psyche, to the emotions, will take the experiences of life, too, into greater depths of soul. Men may have richer and also more scientific experiences, but these do not penetrate the man's soul life as deeply as they do in the case of a woman. The whole of the world of her experiences is deeply graven into a woman's soul. Therefore those experiences will have a stronger tendency to work into the organism, to embrace the organism more closely in the future. In this way a woman will through her experiences in one incarnation develop a tendency towards deeper intervention in the organism and thereby towards the formation of the organism itself in the next incarnation. A deep working into and working through the organism will bring forth a male organism. A male organism appears when the forces of the soul desire to be more deeply graven into matter. You can see from this that the woman's experiences in one incarnation result in a male organism in the next incarnation. Occult teaching here shows that there is a connection which lies outside the bounds of morality. For this reason occultism states: man is woman's karma. The male organism of a later incarnation is the result of the experiences and events of a preceding female incarnation. Even at the risk of giving discomfort to some of those present here – after all, many men today are horrified at the thought of incarnating as women – I must state these facts entirely objectively.

Now, how about the experiences specific to men? We shall best understand them if we base them on what has been said before. In the male organism the inner man has penetrated more thoroughly into matter, and has embraced it more closely than in the female. Women retain more of the spiritual in the non-physical sphere. They do not penetrate so deeply into matter, and keep what is physical more flexible. The separation from the spiritual is not as complete. It is characteristic of the female nature that a greater degree of free spirituality is retained, and for that reason women do not penetrate as profoundly into matter, and keep their brains more flexible. Therefore it is not surprising that women have a special inclination for what is new, especially in the spiritual realm, because the spiritual has been retained more freely and because there is less resistance. And it is not by accident, but in accordance with a profound law, that in a movement which in its very nature deals with spirituality, there should be a greater number of women than men. Every man knows that the male brain is frequently an intractable instrument. On account of its rigidity it offers terrible resistance when one wants to use it for more flexible lines of thought. It refuses to follow and it must first be educated by all sorts of means before it can lose its rigidity. Every man will have experienced this.

The nature of the male is more condensed, more concentrated; it has been compressed more, rendered more rigid and hard by his inner being; it has been made more material. Now, a more rigid brain is first and foremost an instrument for the intellectual, rather than for the soul. For intellectuality deals mainly with the physical plane. What might be called the intellectualism of the male is a consequence of a more rigid, more solidified brain. In this respect we might speak of the brain as being 'frozen' to a certain degree. If it is to find its way into subtler trains of thought, it must first be thawed. Therefore a man will be inclined to grasp the external and to absorb less of those experiences that are connected with the depths of his soul life. What he does absorb does not penetrate deeply. We have an external proof of this in the shallowness of external science, and its comparative failure to comprehend the inner being. Although much thought is expended in a wide circumference, facts are concentrated with little thoroughness. Anyone who is compelled by their own discipline of thinking to put the facts together might experience occasional nausea at what is so bluntly presented as objective fact in the field of ordinary science. It becomes quite clear, then, how little depth there is.

Let me quote an example of the superficiality of modern science. Let us suppose a young man is in a college where a rabid Darwinian is lecturing. This is how the advocate of the theory of selection will characterize certain facts: 'Whence does a cock derive his beautiful iridescent feathers of bluish tints?' This is to be traced back to sexual, natural selection; for the cock attracts the hens by his colours, and the hens will choose those from among the cocks who possess these bluish iridescent feathers. In this way the other cocks are ignored, and the consequence is that one particular species is developed. This is progress; this is 'natural selection'! And the student is glad to know how progressive development is brought about.

Then he goes to the next hall, where physiology of the senses is dealt with. It may well happen that the same student in this second hall will hear the following: 'Experiments have been made which show how the various colours of the spectrum affect various beings.' It can be proved that of the whole colour spectrum, hens, for instance, can only see the colours ranging from green to orange, and red to ultra-red, but not those ranging from blue to violet.

Now a student, if he wants to combine these two facts, which really are taught today, is forced to take things superficially. The whole of the theory of natural selection is based on the hens perceiving the cock's variegated colours which is supposed to give them special pleasure, but which they don't see in reality, for the colours appear raven-black to them.

This is merely an example, but anyone willing to investigate really scientifically will encounter instances of this kind wherever he goes. This will demonstrate that intellectuality does not penetrate very deeply into life but remains on the surface. I deliberately chose crass examples.

You might find it hard to believe that intellectuality is something that tends to take place on the surface, and does not work deeply into the life of the soul, hardly takes hold of man's inner being. And the materialistic frame of mind takes even less hold of the soul. The consequence of this is that an incarnation in which little has penetrated into the soul will bring forth a tendency between birth and death to penetrate less deeply into the organism in the next incarnation. After all, the individuality would have taken up less strength to do this; that is why it now results in the human being penetrating less deeply into his body. So comes the inclination to build up a female body in the next incarnation, and it is therefore correct when occultism says: woman is man's karma!

We can see in this morally neutral sphere that what we prepare in one incarnation will organize our corporeality in the next. And as these things not only affect our inner life profoundly but also affect how we experience things and what we do, the following is true: a human being's experience as a man or a woman in one incarnation will determine what this person will do outwardly in the next; the female experience will produce an inclination to build a male organism and the male experience will produce an inclination to build a female organism. Incarnations in the same sex rarely succeed one another; at the most it can happen seven times. However, as a rule, the male organism will strive to become female in the next incarnation, and vice versa. No amount of personal dislike will change these matters, as it is not a question of what we want in the physical world but solely a matter of the tendencies developed between death and a new birth; and these are determined on more sensible grounds than the fact that someone incarnated as a man might experience horror at the thought of incarnating as a woman next time round. You can see how one life is karmically determined by the preceding one and how this equally affects what we do in life.

Now we need to look into yet another karmic connection in order to gain a clearer idea of the fundamental questions we will consider in the next few days.

Let us look back once more to a rather distant time in human evolution, the time when human beings began to incarnate on earth. This happened in the ancient Lemurian epoch. I would ask you to recall that at first the luciferic influence worked deeply into man, and then called forth the ahrimanic influence. Try and present before your souls how the luciferic influence affected human life externally. The very fact that man attained the capacity to absorb the luciferic influence in those ancient times, in other words, to permeate his astral body with the luciferic influence, had the effect that his astral body was inclined to penetrate far more deeply into the organism, into the material part of the physical body, and to do so in quite a different way. Through the luciferic influence the human being became more material. Without this influence the human tendency to descend into the material world would have been far weaker, and man would have remained in higher spheres of existence. In other words, his outer and his inner aspects became more strongly united than they would have been without the luciferic influence. The first effect of this more intimate connection with the material physical body was that we lost the ability to remember what happened before we took up our physical body. We entered existence by way of birth which strongly tied us to matter; this effaced all memory of earlier experiences. The luciferic influence made birth into an act through which our physical aspect becomes so intimately connected with the spiritual aspect that everything experienced in the spiritual world before birth is effaced. The luciferic influence robbed us of our memory of earlier spiritual experiences. It is due to this connection with the outer physical body that we cannot look back on what happened before. That is why we depend in our life on gaining knowledge and experience from the outer world.

However, it would be totally wrong to believe that we are only affected by the coarse outer substances we absorb. Besides the food we eat and the forces connected with such nutrition, all our experiences, too, affect us, even the things that flow into us through our senses. But through this coarser connection with matter the foods, too, work differently. Imagine that the luciferic influence had not occurred; then everything – from the food we eat to the impressions of our senses – would work into us in a far more subtle way. We would be able to imbue everything we experience by interacting with the outside world with our experiences between death and birth. Because of the greater condensation of the physical we also tend to absorb what is denser.

This is the work of the luciferic influence: through the condensation of matter the human being draws much denser matter from the world outside. This denser matter which he draws in from outside is of a very different quality than the otherwise less dense substance. The lower degree of density would have enabled us to retain our memories of our earlier existence; a further effect would be a sense of certainty that everything we experience between birth and death has repercussions into infinity. We would know for certain: 'It's true that outwardly death takes place, but everything that happens carries on working.' Because we had to absorb denser matter we brought about an intense interaction between our bodily nature and the world around us from the time of our birth onward.

What is the effect of this state of interaction? All memory of the spiritual world is eclipsed from the time of our birth. And to enable us to live in the spiritual, to wake up in the spiritual world, that state has to be restored where all that has entered into us as denser matter from outside must be taken from us again. To re-enter the spiritual world we must wait for the time when the outer material body is taken from us. That which enters us as denser matter from the time we are born destroys our human corporeality step by step. Our bodily matter is gradually destroyed by all that enters us in this way until the destruction is so complete that the body can exist no longer. From the time we are born we take up matter which is of greater density than we would have done without the luciferic influence; we slowly destroy our body until it is totally unusable; this is when death occurs.

This shows us that the luciferic influence is the karmic cause of human death. If human beings were not born in this way they could not die in this way, or else we would face death with a certain prospect of what is to come. Death is the karmic consequence of birth, birth and death are linked by karma. Without the kind of birth we experience today there would not be death as we experience it today.

As I have said already, we cannot refer to karma in relation to the animal as we do in relation to man. If someone stated that even for the animal birth and death are karmically linked he would only show that he is not aware of the very different quality of human death and animal death. What might look similar from the outside is not the same within; it is the inner experience and not the outer event which is significant in birth and death. In the case of an animal only the generic soul or group soul experiences what takes place. For the group soul the death of an animal is approximately the same as what you experience when you have your hair cut at the beginning of summer; your hair will then slowly grow back. The group soul of an animal species experiences an animal's dying like the dying off of a limb which will gradually be replaced again. We can compare the group soul to the human 'I'. It doesn't know birth or death and has an uninterrupted awareness of what precedes birth and of what follows death. To speak of an animal's birth and death in the same way as we speak of man's would be absurd, as they are preceded by quite different causes. We would deny the inner activity of the spirit if we were to assume that what appears identical on the outside must be brought about by identical inner causes. Identity of outer processes doesn't necessarily point to identical inner causes. The birth of a human being rests on very different causes than that of an animal, and likewise human beings die for very different reasons from animals.

That this is so can be ascertained methodologically by just mulling over for a bit how things can be identical outside and not be remotely the same inside. It is extremely simple to find out that what you perceive with your senses is no proof of what goes on inside. Think of two people; you arrive at a particular place at nine o'clock and see these two people standing next to each other. At three o'clock you return to that place, having not been there in the meantime. You see the two people standing at the identical spot again. Now you might conclude: A is still at the same spot, B is still at the same spot, exactly where they were at nine o'clock. However, if you were to examine what these people have done in the meantime you might find that one stayed at the spot while the other had taken a long walk in the meantime and got tired. What you see has been caused by totally different processes. It would be nonsense to say that the two people must have had identical inner experiences because they are standing at the same spot again at three o'clock; and it is equally nonsense to conclude from the identical structure of two cells of the same shape that their inner meaning is one and the same. What is important is to know the overall context of facts which have resulted in a particular cell arriving at a particular place. That is why modern cell physiology, which is based on analysing the inner cell structure, is utterly misguided. What we are able to perceive with our physical senses can never ever be proof of the inner nature of the phenomenon concerned.

Anyone who wishes to grasp what may be derived from occult observation, such as the fact that being born or dying is fundamentally different in the human being from what it is in the mammal or even in birds, will have to think these things through properly. It will only be possible to study these things properly when a little more attention is paid again to what spiritual research yields in these matters. As long as this is not the case, natural science – which stops at the sense perceptible and the external – will certainly bring to light all sorts of wonderful facts; yet whatever human beings may bring forth about such facts under these circumstances will never relate to reality. This is why all that constitutes today's theoretical science is a figment of imagination, utter fantasy, brought about through correlating outer facts on the basis of their outer appearance. In many areas it is the outer facts and circumstances themselves that urge us to interpret them correctly; yet the general approach adopted today will not make it happen.

Now we have considered two neutral issues that relate to the laws of karma and you will find this a useful background to our further studies. We have learned that the female organism is the karmic consequence of experiencing life as a man and that the male organism is the karmic consequence of experiencing life as a woman; and finally we grasped that death is the karmic effect of birth in human life. If you endeavour gradually to deepen your understanding of these things you may attain deep insights into the karmic connections of human life.

LECTURE 10

Free Will and Karma in the Future of Human Evolution

Hamburg, 27 May 1910

There are certain far-reaching questions of karma which are difficult to answer or even approach in any way without touching on certain important mysteries of our world existence, and this I intend to do today. These questions mainly relate to our ability to influence karma, especially other people's karma – in other words to the possibility of changing the direction of karma to a greater or lesser extent. Such questions may arise or else be resolved out of what has been said and illuminated from different angles, or followed through in other ways.

We might ask what happens in a person's karma when by reason of his previous acts or experiences a necessity for illness has arisen to compensate for these acts and experiences, and this person is actually healed through human assistance by means of remedies or other intervention. What does this signify and how does it relate to an in-depth view of the law of karma?

I will say right away that in order to deal with just a few of the major points of this question I will need to touch on things that are very far removed from today's scientific thinking as well as from the general concepts held by people in our time; things that can only be discussed among anthroposophists, as it were, who are prepared for it in the sense of already having

acquired some knowledge about the deeper grounds of existence and who also have some idea of the deeper reasons
behind the phenomena which can only be dealt with in
outline today. Nevertheless I would like to take this opportunity to ask one thing of you.

I will have to talk about the deeper foundations of the
earth's existence today and I shall endeavour to express
myself as precisely as possible. But it would be wrong to
speak in this way in a different context or out of context, and
it would lead to one misunderstanding after another. I ask you
for the present time just to accept it, and make no other use
of it. I, too, must therefore insist with regard to these things
that no one should consider them as teachings which could
simply be passed on in some way or other, for it is only the
context which justifies such a presentation; and such a
presentation is only justified when it is backed by the consciousness that can coin suitable words to express thoughts of
this kind.

We are going to be concerned with the deeper nature of
material existence on the one hand, and the nature of soul
existence on the other. It is essential that we acquire a deeper
comprehension of what pertains to the soul and to the material
world. This is, indeed, necessary for a quite definite reason –
for the reason given in the previous lectures when we said that
the human soul can penetrate more or less deeply into matter.
Yesterday we characterized the nature of the male by saying
that in a man the soul penetrates deeper into matter, while in the
female the soul holds back in a certain way and is more
independent of matter. We saw that much of karmic experience depends upon how the penetration of the soul into matter
takes place. We saw also how certain illnesses in one incarnation appear as the karmic consequences of errors made by the
soul in former incarnations when it worked at its deeds,

experiences and impulses. Then on the way between death and a new birth the soul acquired the tendency to transform into matter that which was formerly only as a characteristic, a mere influence in the soul, so that it now permeates the body. Because the human being is then permeated by a soul which has also absorbed either the luciferic or ahrimanic influence, the human substance is damaged in consequence. This is where the illness takes its course. So we can say: 'In a sick body there dwells a damaged soul which has come under a wrong influence – a luciferic or ahrimanic influence; as soon as these influences are diverted from the soul the normal relationship of soul and body should come about; in other words, health would be restored.' So we must ask ourselves: 'What are these two principles of human existence on earth, matter and soul; what is their deeper nature?'

Nowadays people generally imagine that the answer to the questions: 'Of what does matter consist? What is the soul?' would have to be the same all over the world; and I am not suggesting that human beings should find it easy to grasp that the beings who lived on the old Moon would have answered the question about the nature of matter and soul very differently from earthly beings. For existence is so much in the throes of evolution, that even things like the ideas a being may have about the deeper foundations of his own nature will change; so that the answer to the questions 'What is matter? What is the soul?' must also change. Therefore it must be clear from the start that any answers given are answers of earthly beings, and relevant only to earthly beings.

A person will at first judge 'matter' according to what confronts him in the external world in the shape of different beings and things, and everything which makes an impression upon him in any way. Then he discovers that there are different sorts of matter. But I need not go very far into that, for you may find in all the ordinary books those expositions which could be given here if we had more time. These differences in matter present themselves to us when we see the different metals, gold, copper, lead, and so on, or when we see anything that does not belong to this category. You know, too, that chemistry traces these different materials back to certain fundamental substances of matter, called elements. These elements, even in the nineteenth century, were still considered to be substances possessing certain properties which did not admit of being further divided. But in the case of a substance such as water, we are able to separate it into hydrogen and oxygen, yet in hydrogen and oxygen themselves we have substances which, according to the chemistry of the nineteenth century, were incapable of being further divided. One could distinguish about seventy such elements. You will doubtless also know that owing to phenomena which were produced in connection with a few special elements – radium, for instance – and also owing to various phenomena produced in the study of electricity, the idea of the elements has been shaken in many ways. Then it was concluded that the seventy elements or so were only temporary limitations of matter, and that one could trace back the possibility of subdivision to a fundamental substance, which then, through inner combinations, through the nature of its inner elementary being, manifests at one time as gold, at another time as potassium, calcium, and so on.

These scientific theories vary; and just as the scientific theories changed in 'each fifty years' of the nineteenth century, so it came about that certain physicists saw in matter certain entities which are charged with electricity. Just as the theory of ions is now in fashion there will be other fashions in science in the not too distant future, and other theories about the constitution of matter. These are facts. Scientific opinions are changeable, and must be changeable, for they depend altogether upon those facts which are of significance for one particular epoch. In contrast to this, the teachings of spiritual science have always and throughout all epochs of earthly civilization embraced one and the same view about the nature of material existence, about matter; and this will be true for all future earthly civilizations. In order to lead you on to what spiritual science looks upon as the essence of matter, I should like to say the following:

You all know that ice is a solid body – not through its own nature, but through external circumstances. It at once ceases to be a solid if we raise the temperature sufficiently; it then becomes a fluid substance. Therefore it does not depend upon what is in a substance itself as to what form it takes in the external world, but upon the entire conditions of the universe surrounding it. We can then further bring heat to this substance, and out of the water we can, after a certain point, produce steam. We have ice, water, steam, and through the raising of the temperature we have caused what we may describe as 'the appearance of matter in manifold forms'. Thus we have to distinguish in matter that the appearance it presents to us does not come out of an inner constitution, but that the manner in which it confronts us depends upon the general constitution of the universe, and that one must not isolate any part of the whole universe into individual substances.

The methods of modern science cannot reach where spiritual science is able to reach. The science of today can never, by means of the methods at its disposal, bring the substance of ice – which, when the temperature is increased, is first made fluid and then turned into steam – into the final condition attainable on earth, into which every substance can be transmuted. It is not possible today, by scientific means, to produce a set of circumstances to demonstrate, for example, the following: If you take gold and rarefy it as far as it can be rarefied upon the earth, you will finally reduce it to one state or another. If you subject silver to the same process, the same will apply; equally with copper, and so forth. Spiritual science can do this because it is based upon the methods of clairvoyant research; and is thus able to observe how, in the spaces between our substances, there is always a uniform substance everywhere which represents the extreme limit to which all matter is reducible. Spiritual research discovers a condition of dissolution in which all materials are reduced to a common basis, but what then appears there is no longer matter, but something which lies beyond all the specialized forms of matter around us. Every single substance, be it gold, silver, or any other substance, is there seen to be a condensation of this fundamental substance, which is really no longer matter. There is a fundamental essence of our material earth existence out of which all matter only comes into being by a condensing process, and to the question: 'What is this fundamental substance of our earth existence', spiritual science gives the answer: 'Every substance upon the earth is condensed light'. There is nothing in material existence in any form whatever which is anything but condensed light. When you know the facts there is no need to prove theories such as the vibration hypothesis of the nineteenth century, when it was attempted to represent light by means coarser than light. Light cannot be traced back to anything else in our material existence. Wherever you reach out and touch a substance, there you have condensed, compressed light. All matter is, in its essence, light.

We have now looked at one side of the question from the point of view of spiritual science. We have seen that light is the foundation of all material existence. If we look at the material human body, that also, inasmuch as it consists of matter, is nothing but a substance woven out of light. Inasmuch as man is a material being, he is composed of light.

Let us now consider the other question: Of what does the soul consist? If we applied the methods of spiritual-scientific research to the actual basic essence of the soul we would find that everything that manifests on earth as a phenomenon of soul is a modification, is one of the infinite variety of transformations possible, of that which we call love, provided that we genuinely grasp the intrinsic meaning of this word. Every single stirring of the soul, wherever it occurs, is love modified in some way or other. And when the inner and outer are configured into one, as it were, and imprinted into one another, as is the case in the human being, we find that his outer corporeality is woven out of light and that his inner soul is spiritually woven out of love. Indeed, love and light are interwoven in some way in all the phenomena of our earth existence. For a spiritual understanding of these matters the first question to ask is this: 'How are love and light interwoven in any way?'

Love and light are the two elements, the two components, which permeate all earthly existence: love as the soul constituent of earthly being, light as the outer material constituent of earthly being.

However, for these two elements, which otherwise would exist separately throughout the great course of world existence, to become interwoven, a mediating force is needed that will weave light into love. The power that thus weaves light into the element of love must have no special interest in love; it must be interested only in spreading the light as far as possible, in letting the light stream into the element of love. Such a power cannot be an earthly power, for the earth is the cosmos of love. The earth's mission is to weave love into everything. In other words, everything which is connected with earthly existence is connected with love in some way.

This is where the luciferic beings come into play. They remained behind on the Moon, the cosmos of wisdom. They have a special interest in weaving light into love. The luciferic beings are at work wherever and whenever our inner soul, which is woven out of love, enters into any kind of relationship with the element of light in any form; and we are, after all, confronted with light in all material existence. When light touches our being in any way whatsoever the luciferic beings appear and the luciferic quality weaves into the element of love. This is how it came about that human beings, over the course of repeated lives, became associated with the luciferic element: Lucifer became interwoven with the element of love; and all that is formed from love has the impress of Lucifer, which alone can bring us what causes love to be not merely a self-abandonment, but permeates it in its innermost being with wisdom. Otherwise, without this wisdom, love would be an impersonal force in us for which we could not be responsible.

But in this way love becomes the essential force of the 'I' where that luciferic element is woven, which otherwise is only to be found outside in matter. Thus it becomes possible for our inner being which, during its earth existence, should receive the attribute of love in its fullness, to be permeated besides by everything that may be described as an activity of Lucifer, and from this side leads to a penetration of external matter; so that which is woven out of light is not interwoven with love alone, but with love that is permeated by Lucifer. When we take up the luciferic element, we interweave into the material part of our own body a soul which is, it is true, woven out of love, but into which the luciferic element is interwoven. It is that love which is permeated with the luciferic element which impregnates matter and is the cause of illness working out from within. In connection with what we have already mentioned as being a necessary conse-quence of an illness proceeding from a luciferic element, we may say that the ensuing pain, which, as we have seen, is a consequence of the luciferic element, shows us the effect of the working of the karmic law. So the consequences of an act or a temptation coming from Lucifer are experienced karmically and the pain itself indicates what should lead to the overcoming of the consequences in question.

Ought we to help in such a case or not? Ought we in any way to remove what has pressed in from the luciferic element with all its consequences working out in pain?

Remembering the answer to our question as to the nature of the soul, it follows of necessity that we have the right to do this only if we find the means, in the case of a person who has the luciferic element in him which caused his illness, to expel that luciferic element in the right way. What is the remedy which exerts a stronger action, so that the luciferic element is driven out? What is it which has been defiled by the luciferic on our earth? It is love! Hence only by means of love can we give real help for karma to work out in the right way. Finally we must see in that element of love, which has been compromised in the soul realm by Lucifer and caused illness, a force which must be affected by another force. We must pour in love. We must give love because that which flows in through a deed of love will be helpful. This element of love given as medicine is common to all those approaches to healing which involve the healing of the soul to a greater or lesser extent. All methods of psychological healing are connected in some way with the administering of love. Love is the medicine we give to the other. Love must be the essence of it all. And it surely can be! Even when the psychology involved is straightforward, when all we do is to help another person deal with his depressed state of mind, love is involved. All methods of healing, from the simplest to the more involved methods of healing which are often referred to, rather amateurishly, as 'magnetic healing', must arise out of love.

What does the healer in such a case actually communicate to the one needing to be healed? It is, to use an expression of physics, an 'exchange of tensions'. What lives in the healer, namely, certain processes in his etheric body, relates in a particular way to the one to be healed, creating a kind of polarity. Polarity arises just as it would in a more abstract sense when one kind of electricity, say positive, is produced and the corresponding other, the negative, appears. In this way polarities are created. This is a supreme deed of sacrifice. We are calling forth a process within ourselves which is not only intended to be meaningful to ourselves, for then one would call forth one process only. In this case, however, the process is intended to call forth in the other the polar opposite. This polarity will depend on the contact established between the healer and the person to be healed; when this is produced, when the opposite process is called forth in the other, this is, in the fullest sense of the word, the sacrifice of a power, the transmuted power of love, a deed of love. This is what works in healing: the transmuted power of love. We must be in no doubt therefore that any endeavour to heal must be carried by this power of love, or else it will fail. Nevertheless, processes of love need not necessarily enter our conscious awareness; they may well take place in the subconscious. Even the techniques of healing, as one might regard them – for example the way the hands are applied – are a reflection of a deed of sacrifice. Even in the case of healing processes where the immediate connections are hidden from us, where we cannot observe what is being done, there is a deed of love involved, even if it has taken on the form of mere technique.

We can see that we may very well intervene by means of soul-related healing – for the reason that the soul essentially consists of love; such healing may appear to involve processes which lie at the periphery of human nature, but it is a fact that that which is love in its essence will be enriched by the love it is in need of. Thus on the one side we see how we can help, so that, after being caught in the toils of Lucifer, the sufferer is able to free himself again. Because love is the fundamental essence of the soul, we may, indeed, influence the direction of karma.

On the other hand, we may ask, what has become of the substance woven from light in which the soul dwells? What has become of the material substance of man that is woven out of light?

Take the body – our outer being in its material corporeality. If through a karmic process there had not been imprinted from out of the soul into matter a love substance such as is permeated by Lucifer or Ahriman; if a pure love substance only had poured in, it would not have been defiling or damaging to the substance woven out of light. If love alone were to flow into matter, it would then so flow into the human body that the latter could not be damaged. It is only because love which has absorbed luciferic or ahrimanic forces can penetrate that the substance woven out of light becomes less perfect than it was originally intended to be. Therefore it is only due to the luciferic or ahrimanic influences which pour into the human being during his consecutive incarnations that the human organization is not what it might be. If it were as it ought to be, it would manifest healthy human substance; but because it has absorbed the activities of Lucifer and Ahriman, sickness and disease result.

How can we remove from outside those influences which have entered from within from an imperfect soul, that is, from a wrong love substance? What happens to the body when something which is inappropriate affects it? According to spiritual science something happens which turns light in some way into its opposite. Light has its opposite in darkness or obscurity. Everything that presents itself – strange as it may sound – as the defilement of that which is woven out of light is a darkness woven out of a luciferic or ahrimanic influence. Thus we see darkness woven into the human substance. But this darkness was only thus interwoven because the human body has become the bearer of the 'I' that lives on through the incarnations. This was formerly not there. Only a *human* body can be subject to this corruption, for such a corruption was formerly not contained in that which was woven out of light.

The human being today draws the basis of his material life out of what he has gradually rejected in the course of evolution – that is, the animal kingdom, the vegetable kingdom and the mineral kingdom. These also contain the different substances woven out of light for earth existence. In none of these substances are there any of the influences which, in the course of human karma, have acted on the organism through the soul. In the three kingdoms around us, therefore, we cannot through luciferic or ahrimanic influence emanating from our love forces have a defiling effect. Nothing of us is there. What in us has been defiled is spread around us in all its purity. Consider a mineral substance, a salt or any other substance which we also have within us, or might have within us. But in us it is interwoven with the love substance defiled by Lucifer or Ahriman. Outside, however, it is pure. Thus every substance outside is distinguished from what it is within the human body. Externally it is always different from what it is in the human being, because in him it is interwoven with the ahrimanic or luciferic influence. That is the reason why, for everything of external substance which can be more or less defiled by us, there must be something outside which represents the same thing in its pure condition without the human damage. That which exists in the world in its purity is the external cure for the corresponding substance in its damaged state. If you apply this in the right way to the human being, you then have the specific remedy for the corresponding injury.

Thus we find in an objective way which remedy may be applied to the human body. Here is the injury characterized as a specific form of darkness – and that which is not yet dark as the outer woven pure light. And we see why we are able to remove the darkness in the human being if we bring pure substance woven from light to bear upon him. Thus the substance woven from pure light is a specific remedy for the injury.

Attention has often been drawn to the fact that anthroposophists in particular should not fall into the narrow-minded error of denying that in such cases there really is a specific remedy against some injury or other, or which beneficially affects one organ or another. It has often been said that the organism has within it the forces with which to help itself. Even though the Vienna School of Nihilistic Therapy may be right in its assertion that by calling up the opposing forces we can bring about a cure, we may nevertheless help the cure by specific remedies. Here we see a parallel which one may describe through spiritual science.

From what I have said about diphtheria, for instance, you may gather that the karmic causes have in this case particularly affected the astral body. We find what is most closely related to the astral body in the animal kingdom. You will always find in those forms of illness closely connected with the astral body that medical science, unconsciously driven by a dim impulse, seeks for remedies which originate in the animal kingdom, whereas the remedies for illnesses whose causes lie in the etheric body are sought for in the vegetable kingdom. An interesting lecture might be given about the relation of the purple foxglove to certain illnesses of the heart. These are things which, inasmuch as they are based on truth, are not right for five years only, as one doctor states, and then begin to be wrong, as in the case when only external symptoms are taken into consideration. But there is a certain treasure of remedies which can always in some way be traced back to some connection with spiritual science, which have been inherited without any knowledge where they came from. Just as today astronomers do not know that the Kant and Laplace theory originated in the mystery schools of the Middle Ages, so people do not know where these really valuable remedies came from. Causes of illness which are connected with the nature of the physical body lead to the use of remedies from the mineral kingdom.

Even such analogies can be helpful indicators. We have established now that our connectedness with the world around us makes it possible for us to be helped in two ways: on the one hand through receiving the modified love inherent in healing methods aimed at our soul-nature, and on the other through one of the many different forms of modified light inherent in physical healing methods. All healing is accomplished with either inner soul-related means, with love, or with outer physical means, which all represent some form of condensed light. One day, when science will have advanced to the stage of taking seriously the supersensible, when it will have been recognized that all matter is a form of condensed light, then this fundamental principle will throw a spiritual light on all scientific searching for outer methods of healing people. Thus we can see that the wisdom accumulated over long periods of time about methods of healing in the mystery schools of ancient Egypt and ancient Greece is not mere nonsense but that there is a sound kernel in all these things. It is not the task of anthroposophy to take sides with any particular school of thought; to say, for instance, that in one school of medicine or another they are administering poison to people! The word 'poison' has an almost suggestive effect these days, and people don't consider that it is altogether relative. What is poison after all? Any substance can work as poison. It depends on the method of healing and on the quantity administered. Water is a strong poison if you drink ten litres of it all at once. The effect of this, in terms of chemistry, is not very different from that of any other substance. It is always a question of the quantity involved, for all these concepts are relative.

From what we have learned today we can say: 'How fortunate that for any illness we may suffer something exists in the world of nature around us which will help us overcome it.' And we can meet the world around us with a special sense that there is more to rejoice over than the delights of beautiful flowers or mountains glowing in the sunlight; we may rejoice over the fact that everything around us is so intimately connected with everything we ourselves are made of, good or bad. We can enjoy a great deal more in nature than that which immediately appeals to us, for we will discover, the more deeply we grasp what it is that has thus condensed into outer matter, that this world of nature in which we delight contains powerful healing substance: the right healing substance for every illness man may succumb to is hidden somewhere in nature. And once we recognize nature as a healer we must try to understand its language, obey what it tells us and act accordingly. This is rarely possible today because mankind has denied the light, and knowledge has been pervaded by darkness. This has made it difficult to listen to the pure language of nature. Therefore we need to be clear about this: that when no help can be given, when an illness cannot be influenced for karmic reasons, this does not imply absolutely that nothing could be done in every case.

This remarkable connectedness of man and nature shows us once again that the whole wide world is one being, and we are part of this being. The keys to countless mysteries of earth existence lie in these words: Matter is woven out of light, the essence of the soul is love. But this applies only to earth existence and not to any other realm of universal existence. Thus we have shown nothing less than that whenever we change the direction of karma in any way we are connecting ourselves with the elements of our earthly existence, with matter woven out of light or with love that has become soul. We have now established that we can be helped from two different sides due to our connectedness with the world around us. We either draw the remedies out of our surroundings, out of the condensed light, or out of our own soul by the healing act of love. We unite ourselves with what is right in every sense upon the earth, when, on the one hand, we unite ourselves with light and on the other with love. All earth conditions are in some way conditions of balance between light and love and everything unhealthy is a disturbance of that balance. If the disturbance is in the realm of love, we can help by applying the power of love ourselves; and if the disturbance is in the realm of light, we can help by trying to find that light in the universe which will dissolve the darkness within us.

These are the basic elements by means of which human beings can provide help in the sense of healing. They demonstrate how everything in earthly life depends on the balance of opposite elements. Light and love are in fact polar opposites and ultimately everything that happens in the realms of soul and matter on earth depends on the way in which these elements weave into one another in our life. Therefore it need not surprise us that, in all the spheres of human life, evolution continues from epoch to epoch with the balance inclining first to one side and then swinging back to the other, so that the course of evolution resembles the surging of waves. It goes down and it goes up, and the disturbed equilibrium is forever balanced by the pendulum swinging this way or that. When you consider that throughout human life the state of equilibrium is disturbed in one direction or another you will find it possible to understand even the most complex processes in civilization. Take a period when certain harmful effects entered into the evolution of mankind because people only contemplated the inner life and neglected the outer, for example, in the Middle Ages. At the high point of mysticism the external remained unheeded and this led to all manner of misconceptions. This was followed by an age in which people could not bear mysticism at all, but directed their gaze to the outer world so as to make the pendulum swing to the opposite side. And then there are the periods of transition from the Middle Ages to modern times. You will find a great variety of such disturbances in the state of equilibrium.

In this connection I would like to point out that an eminent characteristic of many people in our time is reflected in the fact that they have completely forgotten, have lost their connection, to what might be called the consciousness of a supersensible world. Consequently there are great numbers of people today who are oblivious to the existence of a spiritual world and are therefore opposed even to thinking about the possible existence of a spiritual world. In times like this one will always find something like a counterpart of that phenomenon. I would like to characterize this in very straightforward terms.

When there are people on the physical plane who become so enmeshed in the sense-perceptible world that they completely forget the spiritual world, the opposite tendency appears among those souls who are living in the spiritual world between death and a new birth – a tendency which works over from the physical into the spiritual plane – impelling them to occupy themselves with the influences which act out of the spiritual world into the physical. It is this which brings about in the physical world the intervention by souls who are still in that state before birth. These souls work down into the physical world in any way they can, and they are able to work indirectly through people who are open to such influences from the spiritual world. If one is called upon to introduce clarity in matters like this one must not accept everything that purports to be a revelation from a spiritual world. It is not difficult to distinguish the really characteristic cases in which the dead – in order to make the pendulum swing the other way – are anxious to show in a palpable manner that there is indeed a spiritual world. Because there are so many people who are completely in the dark, who have woven so much darkness into the spiritual part of their nature that they know nothing about the spiritual world, there are among the dead many who have a strong desire to work into the physical world. Such things generally occur when nothing is done deliberately to bring them about on the physical plane. The most typical cases are the ones that happen without any special preparation, and just appear, as it were, as messages from the spiritual world. This is the connection between the two phenomena, on the one hand the people who are caught up in materialism, and on the other, the desire on the part of those in the spiritual world to send messages to the physical world.

You will find much proof of these things collected in the book by our friend Ludwig Deinhard, *Das Mysterium des Menschen*.[1] It is a systematic survey of a lot of interesting phenomena. Such accounts are very scattered in today's scientific literature. Therefore it is a good thing to have in this book a collection of these spiritual facts, which are actually very characteristic of one aspect of our age. You will find very aptly described in this book the typical case of a scientist who tried in all sorts of ways to prove the existence of a spiritual world by materialistic methods – I mean the late Frederick Myers – and who after his death was strongly impelled to show mankind by means of communications from the spiritual world and by spiritual means what he had endeavoured to do during his life.[2]

I told you this to illustrate how in the world and in world affairs we see continual disturbances of the balance, followed by efforts to restore the balance.

This continual disturbance and restoration of the balance between the two elements of light and love is fundamental to earth existence; and in human karma, from incarnation to incarnation, both work to restore the disturbed condition. Karma, working its serpentine way through incarnations is just such a disturbed balance, until man, after all his incarnations, shall at last create the final balance which can be reached upon earth. Having fulfilled his mission on earth, he evolves then into a new planetary form.

I have endeavoured to present you with what you need for a deeper understanding of the laws of karma. That is why I have plainly stated the fundamental and mysterious truth: Matter is in reality woven light, and that which belongs to the soul is refined love. These are ancient occult sayings but they will be true for all times to come and will prove fruitful in human evolution, not only for our pursuit of knowledge but also for our work in the world.

LECTURE 11

Individual Karma and Shared Karma

Hamburg, 28 May 1910

A great deal more could be said about the various ways in which karma manifests. However, as this is our last lecture and the time available was bound to be too short for such a wide topic, you will forgive me for not being able to go into greater detail on this occasion or answer any of the questions you may have. But our movement will continue to exist and there will be other opportunities to expand on what we have dealt with in this course of lectures.

It will have come before your minds again and again that the human being experiences karma as something definite, which is working at every moment in his life. At every moment of our life we can look back on what we lived through, what we did, thought and felt in the incarnations preceding our present one. And we will always find that our present destiny, in inner and outer terms, represents a kind of 'life account' with all our wise and well-reasoned deeds on one side and everything incomprehensible, bad and ugly on the other. The surplus which appears on either side at any one time in life signifies the destiny of that moment.

This raises a number of questions. Let us deal with the most obvious one: What is the connection between what people accomplish together, as a community, to what we call the individual karma of a particular person? We have already looked at this question from other points of view. When we look back on some event in history, for instance the Persian wars, you could not possibly assume that this event, looked at from the Greek point of view in the first place, represents something which is solely for the account of the 'book of destiny' of those individuals who were involved on the outer physical plane.[1] Think of all the leaders in the Persian wars, of all the people who sacrificed themselves at that time, think of everything that was done by these people, from the leaders down to the individual men in the Greek legions. Would you ever, if you contemplated an event such as this in a reasonable frame of mind, simply ascribe the deeds of individuals at that time to their personal karmic accounts? You could not possibly do that! For you could not possibly assume that events that pertain to an entire nation or a major part of civilization mean no more than the sum total of all the individual human beings living out their respective karma. When you look at the course of historical evolution it is important to proceed from event to event; then you will find that there is sense and meaning in human evolution itself, and that such events amount to more than individual people's personal karma.

We can contemplate an event such as the Persian wars and ask ourselves what it signifies in humanity's evolution. In the East a certain civilization had developed which was brilliant and full of light in many ways. But there is no light without shadow. We need to be clear about the fact that the entire culture of the East could only be developed by mankind at the cost of certain darker elements entering into that culture, elements which ought not to have been perpetuated in human development. A prominent element of this nature was the tendency of the East to continue expanding by means of physical force. Of course, without this drive for expansion the whole of the eastern civilization would not have come about. One is unthinkable without the other. However, in order that mankind might develop further, the Greek culture, for example, had to develop against a very different background. But the Greek civilization could not have initiated this purely from what it represented itself. It needed certain elements from other places, and it did indeed borrow important elements from the eastern civilization. Various legends about heroic figures who passed from Greece over to the East clearly tell us that the pupils of certain Greek schools had gone over to the East to bring back to the Greeks those treasures of eastern culture which could only have originated in the eastern civilization, but were then nurtured and transformed by the specific character of the Greek people, by what the Greeks themselves had developed. To accomplish that, these treasures had to be purged of their darker element: the urge to press forward to the West purely by means of physical force. The Roman civilization which followed the Greek, and everything else that contributed to the further development of the European peoples, would not have come about if the Greeks had not cleared the way for the further development of eastern culture and beaten back the Persians and what was associated with them. In this way beating back the Asians was a means of purifying what had been created in Asia.

This is the way to consider all sorts of events in world history, and if you proceed in this way you will obtain a striking picture. If, in a cycle of lectures over three or four years, we applied this way of thinking only to what we know about mankind's evolution from historical documents, we would arrive at something we could veritably call a plan in mankind's evolution. We would then look at this plan and say: 'This had to be accomplished; it had its dark sides, and these had to be overcome; what had been accomplished had to be transformed and carried further.'

In this way we would arrive at a plan of mankind's

evolution, and in discussing this plan it would simply not occur to us to say: 'How did it come about that Xerxes or Miltiades or Leonidas had this or that personal karma?'[2] We have to envisage the personal karma of the individual as something that is interwoven with the overall plan of mankind's evolution. There is no other way of grasping the matter. And this is how we go about it in the field of spiritual science. Consequently we need to recognize that all the events making up the plan of humanity's evolution must be considered to be interconnected in a similar way to karmic events in individual human lives. Then the question may arise as to how this overall plan of mankind's evolution is connected with the personal karma of individual people.

Let us first consider what might be termed the destiny of human development as such. When we look back we see how one civilization after another arises, how the development of one people follows that of another. We see further how people upon people acquire one thing or another which is new, how something permanent is retained from all the individual national cultures, but how at the same time whole peoples need to die out in order that their heritage, their individual achievements, may be saved for the corresponding later epochs of human evolution. Then we will understand without difficulty why spiritual science distinguishes between two separate currents in this continuous course of mankind's evolution.

Consider what we might look upon as a progressive current in the entire course of humanity's evolution as a succession of waves, but with each wave carrying forward some of its substance to the succeeding one. We can get an idea of this if we consider the first post-Atlantean civilization, the supreme achievements of Ancient India. However, when we compare this magnificence with the faint echo of it which is contained in the old Vedas, which in all their greatness offer just a faint reflection of the Rishis' deeds and of what spiritual science tells us about the great culture of the Indians, we are bound to say: 'The original greatness of what this people accomplished for mankind was already in decline when people set about preserving this treasure of human culture in those magnificent verses.' However, the initial achievements of Indian civilization flowed into the entire course of mankind's evolution, and this alone made it possible for that to develop later on for which a younger substance was needed in contrast to that of a people grown old. First of all the Indians had to be pushed back to the southern peninsula; then the Zarathustran world view developed in Persia. Think of the greatness of this world view at the time it originated – and how relatively quickly it declined among the very people who created it! We see the same thing happen in Egypt and Chaldea. Then we see the wisdom of the East pass over to Greece, and we see the Greeks beat back what is eastern on the outer physical plane. In the wake of that the cultural achievements of the entire Orient are taken up into the lap of Greece and interwoven with much that had been acquired in other regions of Europe. Out of this a new element of culture was created which made it possible by a very circuitous route to take up the Christian impulse and transplant it into the West. And in this way we would also find a continuous current of civilization following on into later periods, which consists of different successive elements, each representing a continuation of the preceding one and at the same time something new that had to be bestowed upon mankind. But where did that which thus develops further from epoch to epoch actually originate?

Think of everything each nation experiences in its own culture! Think of everything that must have come to pass in each people as a totality of countless individuals' feelings and sensations, of wishes and enthusiasm for what must be deemed the ultimate achievement, and what constituted the character-istic element of the culture concerned! Think of how the souls of the people had to be totally united with what they desired and aspired to in the context of a particular culture! And in addition it was necessary over innumerable centuries of mankind's evolution that the various peoples, in developing the various cultures which succeeded one another, always lived with a kind of illusion – the illusion that every such people regarded the particular achievement of its own civilization as something eternal and imperishable which could never be taken from it. It is only the emergence of this illusion, over and over again, which made possible the devotion of individual peoples to building a civilization, in the belief that what was being created would last for ever. This illusion exists today, too. It is true, we are no longer giving ourselves over to it with quite such abandon and we do not speak of the 'everlasting nature' of this or that culture, but it nevertheless exists in the form of our not thinking things through to the end, neither in small matters nor in more significant ones – in our not paying any attention to it, as it were.

There you have two things that were needed by the various peoples to develop their particular cultures, and it is only in our time that things are beginning to change somewhat. For the first realm of cultural life in which such illusions will no longer appear will be that founded on anthroposophy. It would be a gross misunderstanding if someone who stands on the firm ground of our cultural-spiritual movement were to believe that the forms in which we choose to express what we know, the thoughts we are able to develop at this point, that which we are able to give today out of our anthroposophical thinking, feeling and will, should be everlasting. It would be extremely short-sighted to maintain that people will discuss anthroposophical truths in three thousand years' time as we do today. We know that on account of the conditions of our time we have to cast some of the continuous product of evolution into the forms prevalent today, and that our successors will express and experience these things very differently. Why is this so? The reason for this is similar to that which caused individual people in many different cultures throughout the centuries and millennia to go through experiences which contributed to the overall development of the culture concerned. Think of the countless experiences people went through in ancient Greece and think of what issued from that later as an extract for the whole of mankind! Then you will say: 'There is a lot more to this than just the individual currents concerned. Many things happen for the sake of the one primary current.'

So we must observe two things: first, something that must spring up and die away in order that from this whole a second thing – in quantitative terms the smallest constituent – may survive as something lasting. Only when we realize that two powers, Lucifer and Ahriman, have been active in human evolution ever since personal individual karma has existed, shall we be able to understand the progress of human evolution. For the aim of this plan of human evolution is that finally, when the earth will have attained its goal, those experiences which were gradually embodied into the whole of humanity's evolution out of the different cultures will bear fruit for all the different individuals, no matter what personal destinies they may have gone through. But to see this goal we have to look at the world's evolution in the light of anthroposophy. For we must not deceive ourselves: this goal must be conceived of in the right way, always keeping in mind the intactness and everlasting nature of the human individuality which continues to absorb what humanity as a whole has acquired, as opposed to merging into some kind of nebulous pantheistic unity – and this goal can only be apprehended by a life of soul imbued with anthroposophy.

Therefore, if we look back on earlier civilizations, we can say: 'Ever since human individualities have incarnated, Lucifer and Ahriman have participated in human evolution.' Lucifer seeks to participate in the progressive stream of civilization by entering into human beings' astral bodies, impregnating them with the luciferic impulse. This is Lucifer's activity in the course of mankind's evolution; he works into the human astral bodies. Human beings could never acquire what they are given by Lucifer just from the powers which drive on the progressive stream of cultural evolution, which I have just described to you. If you look at this progressive stream in isolation from the overall course of human development you can see what the normally progressing spirit beings of the Hierarchies bestow upon humanity as ever renewing gifts. Looking up to the Hierarchies we cannot but say: 'The spiritual beings who are developing normally have given the earth what has become mankind's lasting possession; it has been transformed in the course of time, it is true, but it has become our lasting possession. It is like a tree and the pith within it. This is the continuous living stream of progressive civilization.'

The powers that are developing normally could have brought it about that man endowed his 'I' ever more with this progressive enrichment of human evolution. Then only that which brings us further would have flowed in from time to time; we would be filled more and more with the gifts of the spiritual world, and finally, when the earth had reached its goal, it stands to reason that we would be imbued with everything given to us by the spiritual worlds. However, one thing would not be possible: we should not have been able to develop that original and ardent power of striving, that devotion and fiery enthusiasm for all that is created in one age of civilization after another. The same grounds which bring forth every single aspiration, every desire, equally bring forth the aspiration for the great ideals of humanity, the desire to ennoble and beautify human existence, to create art in the successive periods of human civilization. The same grounds which bring forth injurious desires leading to evil also bring forth the striving after the highest that can be accomplished upon earth. And this capacity of the human soul to be enkindled for the highest ideals would not exist if it was not possible on the other hand for this same ardent desire to sink into vice and evil. That this is possible in the evolution of mankind is the work of the luciferic spirits. We must not fail to recognize that together with the possibility of evil the luciferic spirits have brought us freedom, so that we may freely receive what would otherwise simply flow into our souls.

However, we have also found that everything which Lucifer brings about challenges a response by Ahriman. Thus we see Lucifer and all his hosts work in that specific element of the Greek culture that was to be given to humanity as a whole: in the great heroes and artists of Greece. We see Lucifer penetrating into their astral bodies, causing them to be inflamed with passion for what they honour as the highest. Thus the element which is to flow into human evolution through the Greeks becomes the enthusiasm of the entire folk soul. And that is exactly where Lucifer is lodged. And as Lucifer owes his power to the Moon as opposed to the Earth evolution, he challenges Ahriman to come forth; and as Lucifer develops his activity in the successive periods, Ahriman joins in and destroys bit by bit what Lucifer has brought about on earth. The cosmic evolution of man is a continuous interplay between Ahriman and Lucifer. Without

Lucifer's work in human development there would be no passion, no enthusiasm for the progressive stream of human evolution; without Ahriman, who destroys in culture after culture whatever arose from Lucifer's influence and is not part of the progressive stream, Lucifer would simply per-petuate individual cultures ad infinitum. Here you see Luci-fer fulfilling his own karma which is an inevitable conse-quence of his development on the ancient Moon. And from this it follows that Ahriman must always be chained to Lucifer's heels. Ahriman is Lucifer's karmic fulfilment.

This has given us an insight into the karma of higher beings by the example of the ahrimanic and luciferic ones. There, too, karma holds sway. Wherever there are 'I'-individuali-ties, there is karma. Of course, Lucifer and Ahriman, too, are bearers of 'I's, and that is why the effects of their deeds can react upon them. Many of these mysteries will be dealt with in the summer, during the lecture cycle on the biblical story of the Creation.[3] There is just one thing I would like to point out now because it will show you very clearly how infinitely profound each single word really is in the true occult records.

Have you ever wondered why it is that in the Bible's history of the Creation there is this sentence at the end of each day of creation: 'And the Elohim saw the work, and they saw that it was very good', that it was 'of the best'?[4] These are significant words. Why are they there? After all, the sentence itself shows that it is intended to characterize the Elohim which developed on the Moon in the normal manner and whose opponent is Lucifer. It is something characteristic of the Elohim that they saw after each day of creation that it was 'of the best'. It was given for the reason that this was the Elohims' degree of attainment. Upon the Moon they could only see their work as long as they were performing it; they could have no subsequent consciousness of it. That they were able subsequently to look back reflectively upon their work marks a particular stage in the Elohim's consciousness. This only became possible upon the earth. Indeed, their inner nature is revealed by the fact that the element of will thus issues forth from their being: when they looked at the work, they saw that it was very good. These were the Elohim who had completed their work upon the Moon and who, when they looked at it afterwards upon the earth, were able to say: 'It can remain, it is very good!' But for that it was necessary that their development upon the old Moon should be completed.

Now, what about the luciferic beings, in other words those beings whose development on the Moon was not completed? They will equally have to try and look upon their work on the earth, for example their contribution to the ardour and enthusiasm of the Greek civilization. Then they will see how Ahriman has caused it to crumble away, bit by bit! And they will have to say, because they have not completed it: 'They beheld their day's work, and they saw that it was not of the best, that it had to be blotted out!'

That is the great disappointment of the luciferic spirits; they are continually trying to do their work over again, for ever trying to swing the pendulum to the other side – only to find their work destroyed by Ahriman again and again. You must think of it as an ebb and flow in the tide of human evolution, a continuous rousing of new forces by beings higher than ourselves, and the experiencing by them of continual disappointments. This is part of the experience of the luciferic spirits in the earth's evolution. And humanity had to take on this karma because it is the only way we could attain real freedom. Freedom is only possible when we ourselves attain to the highest development of our earthly 'I'. If we reached all our goals at the end of the earth's development because they were given to us, our 'I' could not be free; for from the beginning it was predestined that all the good of the earth's evolution should flow into man. Man could only become free by adding to this 'I' another which is capable of error and is able to swing backwards and forwards between good and evil and strive again and again after that which is the purpose of all earthly evolution. The lower 'I' had to be given us by Lucifer in order that our striving towards the higher 'I' should be our own original deed.

This is what gave us the possibility of free will. Free will is something which we may acquire bit by bit in the course of time, for we are placed into this life in such a way that this possibility of free will is a constant ideal before our minds. Is there, after all, a state of balance in our development when our human will is free? It is never free, because it can succumb to the luciferic and ahrimanic elements at any moment in time; it is not free because every human being retains a very definite impression on having passed through the portal of death, during the ascending part of kamaloca, and possibly over several decades. The main purpose of our life in kamaloca is that we should recognize to what degree we ourselves are imperfect as a result of the imperfect deeds we committed in the world, that we should see step by step in which ways we have become imperfect. This then gives rise to our firm resolve to make good what we have rendered imperfect. This is how we live through kamaloca, adding one intention to another and deciding summarily: 'I must make good everything that I thought and did which lowered me!' We imprint what we feel during that time into our further life and enter into existence through birth with the appropriate intention – and this is how we take on our own karma. Hence we cannot say that we have a free will if we have entered existence through birth. At most we can say that we may approach the ideal of a free will to the degree in which we succeed in mastering the influences of Lucifer and Ahriman. And nothing but knowledge will enable us to master the luciferic and ahrimanic influences. Firstly, self-knowledge, which means that we become increasingly able to recognize – also in our life between birth and death – our weaknesses in all our three soul faculties of thinking, feeling and will. After all, the harder we strive not to succumb to illusion the greater will be the strength of our 'I' to do without Lucifer's influence, and the better we shall be able to decide what degree of devotion the treasures of mankind that have been attained over time really deserve. Secondly, we need knowledge of the outer world to complement our self-knowledge: the two must work together. Self-knowledge and knowledge of the outer world must become part of our being; then we shall be able to be clear about our relationship to Lucifer.

We study anthroposophy in order to gain a clearer idea to what extent all our actions, our inclinations and our passions involve the activity of Lucifer and Ahriman – this is the special feature of our endeavour. What have we done in this series of lectures other than enlighten ourselves about the manifold ways in which luciferic and ahrimanic forces play into our lives! In our time it is appropriate to start enlightening people about the luciferic and ahrimanic forces. Human beings need to be enlightened if they really are to contribute something to the goal of humanity's earth existence. Wherever you look, wherever human beings are feeling and thinking, you can see how far removed humanity still is from being really and truly enlightened about the effects of Lucifer and Ahriman. You will find that the majority of people do not want any such enlightenment at all. You will find a great many people succumb to a certain kind of religious egotism; all they want is the greatest imaginable state of well-being for their own soul. People are not aware that all sorts of gross desires can be associated with this kind of egotism. Nowhere does Lucifer play a greater part in our feelings than when we strive to ascend to the divine from out of our passions and desires, without having had the divine illuminated by the light of knowledge. Do you not believe that Lucifer often has an especially great part to play in the very places where people consider themselves to be striving for the highest? But the forms of expression that are striven for in this way will also be numbered among Lucifer's disappointments. And those who believe that they will be able to maintain one form of spiritual culture or another on the basis of crass desires, and who never tire of preaching that this anthroposophy is so bad because it believes in something new, ought to consider that it does not depend on human will that Ahriman fastens himself to the heels of Lucifer. The forms of religious striving which have arisen in the course of time will, because Ahriman mingles into them, go under again through Lucifer. The progressive stream of human evolution alone will be saved.

We know that during earlier stages of evolution certain beings sacrificed themselves and stayed behind for our sake. We have established that these beings need to live out their karma for our sake so that we may express in a normal way what these beings can bestow on us. Indeed, Jehovah originally gave man the capacity to absorb the 'I' through the divine breath. If only that divine breath had entered which pulsates in our blood, without that which is capable of straying again and again from the gifts of Jehovah's breath, without the luciferic as well as the ahrimanic impulses in it, we would have attained to the actual gift of Jehovah, it is true, but without the differentiation of a free 'I', conscious of self. Thus it is part of the cosmic plan that certain beings remained behind.

We live in an age today where we may indeed look back on many disappointments of Lucifer, but at the same time look forward to a future in which we shall understand with ever greater clarity what the progressive stream of evolution actually is. Anthroposophy will be the instrument for understanding this progressive stream of evolution, so that we may become ever more conscious of Lucifer's influences, ever more capable of recognizing luciferic influences within ourselves; in this way we shall be better equipped consciously to make use of such influences for the good of humanity instead of allowing them to work, as they previously did, as dim impulses of which we are not conscious. The same applies to the ahrimanic influences.

It is appropriate to point out in this connection that we are in the midst of an important stage of humanity's development, namely that epoch where the soul-forces of human beings are actually reversed in a certain respect. Many of you will be aware already that an age is before us in which certain people, certain individuals, will develop soul faculties different from those recognized today. For example, what anthroposophy can state from the results of spiritual-scientific research, namely that the human being possesses an etheric body in addition to his physical body, can today only be perceived by people who have undergone an appropriate methodical training. But there will be people before the middle of the twentieth century – and this is known from reading the Akashic Record[5] – who will have naturally developed the gift of etheric clairvoyance and who, since mankind has reached the epoch in which this will develop as a natural gift, will perceive the etheric body as permeating the physical body and extending beyond it. Just as man, once able to see into the spiritual world, has descended to the merely physical perception and intellectual comprehension of the outer world, so he is gradually beginning now to develop new, but this time *conscious,* capacities which will be added to the old ones. One of these special new faculties I should like to characterize.

There will be people – at first only a few, for only in the course of the next two or three thousand years will these faculties evolve in greater numbers, and these first forerunners will be born before the end of the first half of the twentieth century – who will experience something like the following. These people will have some experience or other and then feel inclined to step back somewhat from what they were involved in. Then they will have a picture before them which arises from the action concerned. First of all they will not recognize it and will not be able to relate it to what they were involved in. But then – they may have heard something or other of spiritual science – they will discover that this picture which appeared to them like a kind of conscious dream-image is the counter-image of their own deed, a picture of what needs to be done in order that the deed actually performed may be karmically fulfilled.

Thus we are indeed approaching an age in which we will not only understand karma from the teachings of spiritual science but will actually begin to perceive karma. Whereas until now karma was for us an obscure impulse, an unspecified longing which could only be fulfilled in the following life, and which could only be transformed into an intention during the life between death and a new birth, we will gradually evolve towards consciously perceiving Lucifer's creations, towards identifying their effects. However, this power of etheric clairvoyance will only be of use to people who have striven after knowledge and self-knowledge. But even in normal circumstances people will perceive the karmic pictures of their actions to an ever greater degree. It will be something which will carry human beings further and further in their development because it will enable them to find out what they still owe to the world, what is left on the debit side of their karma. After all, what makes us unfree is the fact that we do not know what we still owe the world. That is why it is wrong to speak casually of free will in connection with karma. The expression 'free will' in itself is wrong. We should rather say: 'We, as human beings, only become free through enhancing our cognitive faculties and through rising higher and growing closer with the spiritual world. In this way we will be filled more and more with what the spiritual world has to give us and gradually develop into beings capable of mastering our own will.' It is not the will that can become free – it is the human being as a whole who can become free through absorbing the knowledge of the spiritual world.

Thus we look upon Lucifer's disappointments and his deeds and say: 'The foundations for the position we occupy today have been built over thousands of years; if we did not stand where we stand today we could not evolve to freedom. But as we are in a position to enlighten ourselves with regard to Lucifer and Ahriman we are able to relate to these powers in a new way and gather the fruit from what has been accomplished; we can, as it were, take over the work of Lucifer and Ahriman.' However, the deeds of Lucifer, the developments he inspired, which have caused no end of disillusionment, will have to be turned into their opposite if we are to perform them ourselves. Lucifer's deeds were conditional upon creating wishes and desires, upon leading people into the proximity of evil. We have seen what kind of power is needed to oppose Lucifer. If we ourselves are to counteract Lucifer, if we are to manage his affairs in the future, we will only be able to do this with the power of love. Love will be able to take the place of Lucifer's deeds. Indeed it will. And so will that which comes to us from the world outside when we succeed in ever greater measure in dispelling the darkness which we ourselves weave into outer matter. If we manage gradually to remove this darkness, when this darkness lifts and we reach the stage where the ahrimanic influence can be totally overcome, only then will we be in a position to know this earthly world as it really is. Then we will gradually come closer to the kind of knowledge which is today confined to the realms of spiritual science; we shall penetrate to the real essence of matter – to the nature of light. Present-day science is still subject to all sorts of deceptions as to the nature of light. Many believe that we see light with our physical eyes. It is not true. With our physical eyes we do not see light, but merely illuminated bodies; we see these bodies in different colours. We do not see light but we see through the light. All such deceptions will be swept away. This will transform our view of the world which had to be riddled with error under Ahriman's influence; it will be permeated with wisdom. Through penetrating to the light, we ourselves will develop the soul's counterpart of light. The soul's counterpart of light is wisdom.

This is how love and wisdom will enter the human soul. And love and wisdom will make up the practical strength, the vital impulse that should and eventually will grow from the anthroposophical view of the world. Wisdom, which is the inner counterpart of light, wisdom united with love, and love permeated by wisdom will find the right way to react upon that which is immersed in the wisdom of the outer world. If we are to partake to an ever increasing degree in the other half of evolution and overcome Lucifer and Ahriman, we must permeate ourselves with wisdom and love. In developing wisdom and love we shall be developing the very elements which will need to issue from our souls as gifts to those who sacrificed their own development in the first half of the earth's evolution – the luciferic and the ahrimanic powers who thus gave us what we needed to become free. However, one thing must be clear to us: the world is a living thing and the culture we develop must express what is living. We shall gladly and lovingly devote ourselves to building a culture of anthroposophy which will not last for ever; we shall accept this with unbroken enthusiasm and proceed to create with love what formerly we created driven by Lucifer. Because we recognize now that we have to create out of love what we were formerly driven to create by Lucifer's influence, through passions and desires, we will develop all the more love, a superabundance of love. Without such superabundance of love we should not be able to develop culture after culture. Anthroposophy should be something which inspires people to do what is needed in their time with devotion and love, with the same enthusiasm that people developed in earlier times under the influence of Lucifer. We shall no longer harbour the illusion that what we are doing will last for ever. And in creating culture after culture with love and more love we shall create a superabundance of love. This will benefit Lucifer; it will also counterbalance his disappointments. It is up to us to compensate Lucifer for the disappointments he had to suffer by repaying what has been given us.

This is the other aspect of the karma of higher beings – that we develop a power of love which is not confined to humanity alone but which penetrates right into the cosmos. We shall be able to channel this love into beings higher than ourselves, and they will accept this as our offering. It will be a soul sacrifice. This sacrifice in soul will rise up to those who once poured their gifts upon us like the smoke of incense rising up to the spirits in times when human beings still possessed the gifts of the spirit. In those days they were only able to send up the symbolic smoke of sacrifice to the gods. In times to come they will send up streams of love to the spirits and out of this offering of love higher forces will pour down to humankind, which will work, with ever-increasing power, in our physical world, directed by the spiritual world. These will be magical forces in the true sense.

Thus the evolution of mankind encompasses the fulfilment of human karma and the karma of higher beings. We now can grasp how the overall plan of evolution relates to the personal karma of human beings. Let us assume that a superhuman individuality brought something about in the year 1910 which was carried out on the physical plane by a human being; in this way a contact is established between them, and the person is interwoven with the karma of higher beings. This would establish a definite correlation. But then something different streams down to him from the higher worlds, bringing a new element to his life; this would then establish a new item which is added to his karma and will make the pendulum swing this way or that. Thus human karma is fructified by the general karma that streams through the world.

Consider Miltiades, for example, or some other personality. There they stood in the great plan of their people's history, and some karma of higher powers was involved – and there they were, placed at their post! What poured into their personal karmic account was to benefit the whole of humanity, and by fulfilling it, by following up with action and deed, they made it their individual karma. Thus we live and weave into the macrocosm with our personal karma, as microcosms.

We have now reached the end of this course of lectures, although we have by no means exhausted the subject. But this was only to be expected. There are just two things I would like to say to you now. I have given this series of lectures about those very human questions that are so apt to stir our hearts deeply and are at the same time connected with the great destinies of the highest of beings – I have truly given this course from the depths of my soul and I am happy that it was possible for once to speak about this in an anthroposophical circle, among friends who have come here from all directions to devote themselves to the study of these questions. I am speaking these words from the depths of my heart. Those who will be able to attend further courses will find that many of the questions that may have arisen in the context of this cycle of lectures will be answered then. But also those who will not be able to attend the summer courses will have the opportunity later on to talk to me.

Allow me to express my wish once more that that which I have conveyed to you should be more to you than merely abstract knowledge, that it should imbue your thinking, your feeling and your will, your whole life, so that one should be able to see in the anhroposophists who are out in the world something which really represents the profound truth of an-throposophy. Let us endeavour to become true representatives in this way, for only then will the spiritual substance of anthroposophy flow into the world. In the context of our small circles we need to devote ourselves first and foremost to the study of spiritual knowledge. But then the knowledge thus acquired must shape our fundamental attitudes, and determine the way in which we place ourselves into the world. The world will gradually see that it was not in vain that at the turning-point of the twentieth century there lived honest and upright anthroposophists – people who sincerely believed in the power of the spirit, and whose belief afforded them the strength to work for it. Our life, our culture, will advance in leaps and bounds if you yourselves transform what you have received here into your very attitude to life and put it into practice. Nothing will be achieved by trying to convince people! That is not appropriate in our time. For only those who come to anthroposophy out of their hearts' deepest longing will ever be truly convinced; those who do not will not be convinced. This is the inevitable karma of materialism, and it manifests in a spiritual context, too. We have to view these detrimental effects as something against which spiritual science must prove itself as a power of the spirit.

In this way we must give the world what we are able to give it out of the essence of our whole being. When we will have made anthroposophy into an inner force of soul we will be spiritual sources of strength. And whosoever will believe in the supersensible may be absolutely convinced that what we know and feel and do out of anthroposophy works spiritually. It will spread invisibly into the world if we truly make ourselves into a conscious instrument of anthroposophical life.

NOTES

Lecture 1

1   Christopher Columbus (1446-1506). On the importance of his dis-
    covery of Cuba, Haiti and South America, see R. Steiner, *Rhythmen
    im Kosmos und im Menschenwesen* (GA 350), Dornach 1991, lecture
    of 25 June 1923.
2   Thomas Newcomen (1663-1729) was one of the inventors of the
    piston steam-engine which, after design improvements by James
    Watt (1736-1819), became a driving force of industrialization in the
    nineteenth century.
3   Johannes Kepler (1571-1630), mathematician, physicist, astrono-
    mer, developed three laws by which to interpret the dynamics of the
    planetary orbits. Following Copernicus and Tycho Brahe, he placed
    the sun at the centre. See R. Steiner, *The Spiritual Guidance of
    Humanity* (GA 15), Anthroposophic Press, New York 1992; and on
    the three laws *The Relationship of the Diverse Branches of Natural
    Science to Astronomy*, 3rd Science Course (GA 323), Rudolf Steiner
    Research Foundation, California 1989, especially the lectures of 3
    and 4 January 1921.
4   In *De Harmonice Mundi*, preface to the fifth volume.
5   Probably around 1608 in Holland.
6   For all seven evolutions of the Earth, see R. Steiner, *An Outline of
    Esoteric Science* (GA 13). Anthroposophic Press, New York 1997.
7   Re luciferic and ahrimanic beings see R. Steiner, *The Influences of
    Lucifer and Ahriman* (GA 191 & 193), Anthroposophic Press, Hud-
    son 1993. Lucifer tends towards having an expansive inspiring effect
    through grandiose visions, causing people to lose touch with earthly
    reality. Ahriman seeks to harden, materialize and ultimately trap
    humanity within the earthly realm. Both are necessary for the devel-
    opment of humanity.
8   R. Steiner, *An Esoteric Cosmology* (in GA 94), Garber Communica-
    tions, Blauveldt 1987, lecture of 11 June 1906.
9   Re comets, see R. Steiner, *The Christ-Impulse and the Development of
    Ego Consciousness* (GA 116), Anthroposophic Press, New York 1976,
    lectures of 25 October 1909 and 9 March 1910; *The Reappearance of

Christ in the Etheric (GA 118), Anthroposophic Press, New York 1983, lecture of 5 March 1910; *The Spiritual Beings in the Heavenly Bodies and the Kingdoms of Nature* (GA 136), Anthroposophic Press, New York, lecture of 10 April 1912; *Supersensible Man* (GA 231), Anthroposophical Publishing Company, London 1961, lecture of 17 November 1923; *The Relationship of the Diverse Branches of Natural Science to Astronomy*, op. cit., lecture of 18 January 1921; *Mensch und Welt. Das Wirken des Geistes in der Natur. Über das Wesen der Bienen*, (GA 351), Dornach 1988, lectures of 10 and 24 October 1923; *The Evolution of Earth and Man and the Influence of the Stars* (GA 354), Anthroposophic Press, New York, & Rudolf Steiner Press, London 1987, lecture of 13 September 1924.

10 Edmund Halley (1656-1742) was the first to discover a 'periodically returning comet'. See also R. Steiner, *The Christ-Impulse and the Development of Ego-Consciousness*, op. cit., lectures of 25 October 1909 and 9 March 1910.

Lecture 2

1 René Descartes (1596-1650); see the *Discourse of Method*, 5th section, *Traité de l'homme*, and *Primae cogitationes circa generationem animalium*.
2 See R. Steiner, *An Outline of Esoteric Science*, op. cit., chapter 'Cosmic Evolution and the Human Being'.

Lecture 3

1 See R. Steiner, *Das Ewige in der Menschenseele. Unsterblichkeit und Freiheit*, (GA 67), Dornach 1992, lecture of 18 April 1918.

Lecture 4

1 Joseph Dietl (1804-1878), hospital physician in Vienna, focussing primarily on pneumonia; representative of the extreme nihilistic school of thought.
2 Joseph Skoda (1805-1881), professor of medicine of the 'new Vienna School', worked with Carl Rokitansky (1804-1878).
3 See Lecture 1, Note 7.

4   R. Steiner, *Karmic Relationships, Vol.2* (GA 236), Rudolf Steiner
    Press, London 1974.

Lecture 5

1   Frederic Troels-Lund (1840-1921), Danish historian. In his book
    Gesundheit und Krankheit in der Anschauung alter Zeiten, Leipzig
    1901, he devoted a chapter each to the views mentioned here. Rudolf
    Steiner had this book in his library.
2   Possibly Voltaire.
3   Galileo Galilei (1564-1642), Italian physicist, mathematician and
    astronomer.
4   Martin Luther (1483-1546), inaugurated the Reformation in Ger-
    many. See R. Steiner, *The Karma of Materialism*, Anthroposophic
    Press, New York 1985, lectures of 11 and 18 September 1917.

Lecture 6

1   J. S. Bach (1685-1750), the greatest of many composers in the
    Thuringian 'family of musicians'. See R. Steiner, *The Inner Nature
    of Music* (GA 283), Anthroposophic Press, New York 1983.
2   Meister Eckhart (1250-1327), Dominican, eminent thinker, German
    mystic; accused of heresy in the last year of his life. Johannes Tauler
    (c.1300-1361), Dominican, pupil of Meister Eckhart. Regarding
    these and mysticism in general, see R. Steiner, *Mysticism at the Dawn
    of the Modern Age* (GA 7) Garber Communications, New York 1980.
3   The *Theologia Germanica* was published by Franz Pfeiffer (revised
    edition 1855).
4   Galatians 2, 20.
5   R. Steiner, *An Outline of Esoteric Science*, op. cit.
6   R. Steiner, *Cosmic Memory* (GA 11), Garber Communications, New
    York 1990.

Lecture 7

1   Genesis 3.
2   See R. Steiner, *Cosmic Memory*, op. cit., 'Life on the Moon', and *An
    Outline of Esoteric Science*, op. cit., 'Cosmic Evolution and the

Human Being'.

Lecture 8

1 See R. Steiner, *The Study of Man* (GA 293), Rudolf Steiner Press, London 1990, lecture of 30 August 1919.
2 Charlemagne (742-814), king of the Franks and first Carolingian emperor.
3 Aristotle (384-322BC), pupil of Plato, teacher of Alexander the Great. Especially his works on logic were of fundamental importance to the development of western culture and science.
4 See Lecture 5, Note 4.
5 See R. Steiner, *Karmic Relationships*, Vol.2 (GA 236), Rudolf Steiner Press, London 1974, lectures of 27 and 29 June 1924.
6 See R. Steiner, *Karmic Relationships*, Vol.2 (GA 238), Rudolf Steiner Press, London 1983, lecture of 18 September 1924.
7 See Lecture 1, Note 3.

Lecture 9

1 R. Steiner, *The Reappearance of Christ in the Etheric*, op. cit., lecture of 5 March 1910.

Lecture 10

1 Ludwig Deinhard (1847-1917), engineer and industrialist. With Hubbe-Schleiden he headed one of the first groups of the German Theosophical Society (1894-96). Having campaigned for a German Section of that Society, he subsequently allied himself increasingly with Rudolf Steiner. Steiner thought very highly of his book *Das Mysterium des Menschen im Lichte der psychischen Forschung. Eine Einführung in den Okkultismus*, Berlin 1910. See also R. Steiner, *Mitteleuropa zwischen Ost und West* (GA 174a), Dornach 1982, lecture of 19 May 1917; and *Zur Geschichte und aus den Inhalten der ersten Abteilung der Esoterischen Schule 1904-1914* (GA 264), Dornach 1996.
2 Frederick W. H. Myers (1843-1901), poet, spiritualist, author and friend of Sir Oliver Lodge; in 1882 one of the founders of the Society

for Psychical Research in London. Steiner spoke in detail about his own experiences in connection with Oliver Lodge in *The Karma of Vocation* (GA 172), Anthroposophic Press, New York 1984, lecture of 27 November 1916.

Lecture 11

1   In the Persian wars (490-449BC), the Persians, although outnumbering the Greeks (led by Miltiades) tenfold, were beaten by them at Marathon in 490BC. The fleet of the Persian king, Xerxes, was defeated at Salamis in 480BC.
2   Xerxes (c.520-455BC), Persian king, launched a campaign against Hellas in retaliation for his father's defeat at Marathon. He forced a passage through the narrow pass of Thermopylae, which was occupied by Leonidas, but was defeated at the Battle of Salamis in 480BC. Miltiades (died c.488BC), Athenian general, defeated the Persians at Marathon in 490BC. Leonidas (d. 480BC), Spartan king, died in battle against Xerxes at Thermopylae.
3   R. Steiner, *Genesis* (GA 122), Rudolf Steiner Press, London 1982, 11 lectures 16-26 August 1910.
4   Genesis, 1, 31.
5   The history and evolution of the earth and all its inhabitants is retained in the earth's 'etheric' or life body and can be 'read' as the Akashic Record by someone who has acquired the necessary faculty. See R. Steiner, *Cosmic Memory*, op. cit.

Publisher's Note Regarding
Rudolf Steiner's Lectures

The lectures and addresses contained in this volume have been translated from the German, which is based on stenographic and other recorded texts that were in most cases never seen or revised by the lecturer. Hence, due to human errors in hearing and transcription, they may contain mistakes and faulty passages. Every effort has been made to ensure that this is not the case. Some of the lectures were given to audiences more familiar with anthroposophy; these are the so-called 'private' or 'members' lectures. Other lectures, like the written works, were intended for the general public. The difference between these, as Rudolf Steiner indicates in his *Autobiography*, is twofold. On the one hand, the lectures given to members of the Anthroposophical Society take for granted a background in and commitment to anthroposophy; in the public lectures this was not the case. At the same time, the members' lectures address the concerns and dilemmas of the members, while the public work speaks directly out of Steiner's own understanding of universal needs. Nevertheless, as Rudolf Steiner stresses: 'Nothing was ever said that was not solely the result of my direct experience of the growing content of anthroposophy. There was never any question of concessions to the prejudices and preferences of the members. Whoever reads these privately printed lectures can take them to represent anthroposophy in the fullest sense. Thus it was possible without hesitation – when the complaints in this direction became too persistent – to depart from the custom of circulating this material "for members only". But it must be borne in mind that faulty passages do occur in these reports not revised by myself.' Earlier in the same chapter, he states: 'Had I been able to correct them [the private lectures], the restriction *for members only* would have been unnecessary from the beginning.'